TOMMY'S TEAM

THE PEOPLE BEHIND THE DOUGLAS YEARS

STUART HOUSTON and BILL WAISER

FIFTH HOUSE

Published by Fifth House Ltd.
A Fitzhenry & Whiteside Company
195 Allstate Parkway
Markham, ON L3R 4T8
www.fifthhousepublishers.ca

Library and Archives Canada Cataloguing in Publication Data
Houston, Stuart
Tommy's team : the people behind the Douglas years / Stuart Houston and Bill Waiser.

Includes index.
ISBN 978-1-897252-75-8

1. Douglas, T. C. (Thomas Clement), 1904-1986--Friends and associates.
2. Saskatchewan--Politics and government--1944-1964. 3. Canada--Politics and government--1935-. 4. Premiers (Canada)--Saskatchewan--Staff--Biography. 5. Social reformers--Canada--Biography. 6. Politicians--Saskatchewan--Biography. 7. Politicians--Canada--Biography. 8. Saskatchewan-- Biography. I. Waiser, W. A II. Title.

FC3525.1.D68H68 2010   971.24'030922 C2010-902211-4

The publisher gratefully acknowledges the support of the Canada Council for the Arts and the Department of Canadian Heritage and the Ontario Arts Council. We acknowledge the financial support of the Government of Canada through the Book Publishing Industry Development Program (BPIDP) for our publishing program.

Cover and interior design by BookWorks
Front cover image Murray Mosher Photography

Printed in Canada
10 9 8 7 6 5 4 3 2 1

Contents

Introduction

On 29 November 2004, T. C. (Tommy) Douglas easily topped a month-long, national Canadian Broadcasting Corporation television poll as "The Greatest Canadian." It is easy to understand why. The recognition was largely a consequence of Tommy's preeminent role in the introduction of medicare in the 1960s, what many citizens regard today as a defining feature of Canada, and one many are prepared to fight to maintain.

But Tommy Douglas was much more than the "Father of Medicare." He made many other contributions to Canadian life, most of them during his seventeen-year tenure as Saskatchewan's first Co-operative Commonwealth Federation premier (1944–61). He also did not accomplish all that he did on his own and would have been the first to admit it. Regrettably, though, the people who helped make these contributions possible or helped bring them to fruition have been largely overlooked, forgotten, or simply ignored—ironically, in large part, because of the tendency to focus on Douglas. The diminutive Tommy tends to cast a large shadow over the CCF government and its accomplishments, as evidenced by the existing biographies or the recent CBC television production, "Prairie Giant."

That's what makes this book so different. *Tommy's Team: The People Behind the Douglas Years* offers an unprecedented look at the people who played a significant, and often influential, role in his life and career up until he decided to step down as Saskatchewan premier in 1961. All of these individuals are interesting in their own right, but it is the connection to Tommy that shapes and informs the collection. The research for the book has unearthed a good deal of fascinating, sometimes surprising, information about these people and their relationship with Douglas. The result is a collection of essays that provides a broader, at times more nuanced, perspective on Douglas and helps explain why he was one of the most successful political leaders of his era and why his government left such a lasting legacy.

With the exception of Stanley Knowles, Tommy Douglas's competitor for the church pulpit in Weyburn, the book deliberately excludes his political colleagues, who rightly belong in political histories and biographies. Instead, it examines the contributions of individuals who never held political office but were nonetheless important players before and during his years as North America's first social democratic premier. Among them are the Winnipeg doctor who saved Tommy's leg from amputation and provided Douglas with the inspiration for medicare; the Weyburn storekeeper, an ardent Liberal, who opened the way for Tommy to preach at Calvary Baptist Church; the storekeeper's daughter who turned her back on her family's Liberal leanings and went to work as Tommy's executive secretary for nearly four decades; the Japanese-Canadian evacuee who became Tommy's foremost economic advisor; and the son of impoverished Ukrainian immigrants who spearheaded the introduction of medicare in the Swift Current region sixteen years before the provincial plan.

The biographical essays that follow are presented in alphabetical order by surname. This arrangement is deliberate, in that it allows readers to dip into the collection here and there—at their whim—and gain some understanding and appreciation of the parade of people who helped make the Douglas premiership one of the most exciting periods in Saskatchewan history and the Regina capital one of the most vibrant places to be in Canada at the time. The essays also underscore Tommy's uncanny knack for choosing the right person for the task at hand. Despite his lifelong idealism and socialist leanings,

Douglas was both realistic and practical. Finally, the essays provide insight into the formative influences on Douglas, some of them serendipitous, and help explain why he came to power in 1944 with a clear sense of where he wanted to take the province.

Tommy Douglas and his achievements have long been recognized. It is time to turn the spotlight on the people behind the stage and in the wings. This book is their curtain call.

Bill Baker

When the Tommy Douglas CCF government assumed power in Saskatchewan in 1944, it seemed that the largely rural, agriculturally based province was out-of-step with the rest of the country. The new Canada was an urban, modern, affluent place, whereas Saskatchewan was seen as backward, lacking in opportunity, but worst of all, in decline.

Premier Douglas wanted to secure the future of rural Saskatchewan—to take whatever steps were required to improve rural services and place agriculture and the family farm on a more stable footing. But before this revitalization could get underway, there needed to be a better understanding of the challenges that rural Saskatchewan faced in the post-war world.

The CCF government consequently called on Bill Baker, professor of Rural Education at the University of Saskatchewan, to head a provincial royal commission into agriculture and rural life. While royal commissions are often cynically regarded as a way for governments to delay taking action, Douglas expected Baker's team to come up with a blueprint for rural revitalization as soon as possible. The premier found it personally difficult to watch the commission's work from the sidelines, knowing that the change that was occurring in the countryside would not wait.

The Royal Commission on Agriculture and Rural Life quickly became known as the "people's commission" because of chairperson Bill Baker's insistence on involving the public as much as possible. SASKATCHEWAN ARCHIVES BOARD S-B4780

William Bernard Baker was born in Veregin, Saskatchewan, on 1 January 1919—a New Year's baby—and raised on the family mixed farm. He entered the University of Saskatchewan School of Agriculture in 1938, transferred to the degree program after two years, and graduated with a Bachelor of Science in Agriculture, with a specialty in farm management, in 1944.

Baker did part-time graduate work in rural sociology at the universities of Minnesota, Kentucky, and Michigan over the next eight years, but never completed his doctorate. That's probably because he was serving, at the same time, as director of the Saskatchewan School of Agriculture. His graduate studies were also sidetracked by a request from Premier Douglas in 1952 to head up a special provincial royal commission on agriculture and rural life.

The idea for the commission originated with Douglas. "I'd had the germ of the idea for many years," the premier explained. "While we knew that this social and economic revolution was taking place, and that there was a shifting pattern of life in the rural areas, nobody had ever tried to plot it."[1] This revolution involved the widespread mechanization of agriculture, the associated movement to larger farms, and the consequent decrease in rural population. The Saskatchewan countryside was losing people at a near-record rate, and it was not clear how this change was going to affect the fabric of rural society, especially since agriculture no longer dominated the Canadian export economy.

Douglas was not interested in piecemeal solutions to rural reconstruction. As Al Johnson, the deputy minister of Finance, commented years later, the premier regarded all past studies of farm problems as "parts of a single puzzle, and he wished to see them put together."[2] He therefore chose the royal commission route—something he first raised with Cabinet in 1951. It was not until after the 1952 provincial election, however, that the terms of reference were announced and the commissioners appointed.

Bill Baker, as a specialist in rural issues, born and raised in rural Saskatchewan, was an obvious candidate to head the commission. But he was also a devoted advocate of adult education, something that matched up well with Douglas's own thinking. "He believed that if adults had access to information they would make wise decisions," a colleague observed, "and [he] strove to improve the methods and processes used to involve the public in decision making."[3] These attitudes were reflected in how Baker ran the commission over the next four years.

The Royal Commission on Agriculture and Rural Life quickly became known as the "people's commission" because of Bill Baker's insistence on involving the public as much as possible.[4] Over the next three years, the commission sponsored eighty community forums and nearly sixty public hearings, and surveyed the opinions of hundreds of rural residents through questionnaires. Briefs were also solicited from various groups and organizations involved in rural Saskatchewan, while the commission staff conducted research on select topics.

Most of the public discussion revolved around the twin issues of distance and isolation and the related problem of rural depopulation. Presenters offered all kinds of solutions, such as directing immigrants to rural areas, limiting the amount of land that farmers could own, and bringing together all the farmsteads in a district into a village-like setting.

The commission issued its first report on the scope and nature of the investigation in March 1955. Thirteen other reports—ranging from agricultural credit and rural education to farm electrification and service centres—regularly followed over the next months until April 1957. Collectively, they could be considered the doctoral dissertation that Baker never finished.

Some of the commission's findings proved quite controversial, such as the recommendation that the family farm be redefined to reflect the new realities of post-war agriculture, or that nine-township rural municipalities that had existed since 1908 be replaced by a county system. Many were also beyond the powers of the provincial government, especially those dealing with the marketing of wheat and farm income.

But what made the commission so important to the province's history—and its future—was that it provided a comprehensive snapshot of a society undergoing fundamental change and the many problems and challenges associated with that change. "The commission said two things must be done," Douglas recounted. "One was to see that people aren't hurt in the process of adjustment, and secondly, that we must direct this adjustment toward desirable social objectives."[5]

Ironically, the CCF government was not prepared to wait until the commission had completed its reporting and went ahead with the plans for rural revitalization. Beginning in the early 1950s, it started building a province-wide network of all-weather roads, expanded and upgraded the provincial telephone service, and began to provide electricity to towns, villages, and thousands of farms. These various measures were all part of the Douglas attempt to provide the same level of services in the countryside as in the province's cities.

But rural leaders pushed back when it came to the reorganization of rural municipalities into larger units. In 1956, when Douglas reported that the government was actively pursuing a new form of local government on the advice of the commission, the president of the Saskatchewan Association of Rural Municipalities accused the premier of secretly plotting to do away with RMs since his first days in office. The vehemence of the attack owed much to the local anger over the closure of rural schools since the end of the war, and although the CCF government tried to defuse the issue by appointing a special committee to find a compromise, the idea was shelved in the face of continuing opposition.[6]

Once the royal commission completed its work, Bill Baker was appointed director of the new Centre for Community Studies at the University of Saskatchewan. In 1964, he was awarded an honorary degree from North Dakota State University largely for his work on the commission, "an outstanding example of the principles of social science applied to practical solutions."[7] This work was also recognized the following year when he was named to the executive of the new National Advisory Council on Rural Development. Baker moved to Ottawa in 1966 when the Saskatoon centre became a national organization. He died there three years later at the age of fifty.

As for the royal commission, it could do little to restore the once-vibrant rural society, let alone halt rural decline in Saskatchewan over the next few decades. But it was an unprecedented success in participatory democracy by giving people a voice in the commission's investigations, "a breakthrough in the art of government in Canada."[8]

Bill Baker certainly appreciated the significance of his assignment. Writing to the premier one year after the commission had wrapped up its work, he spoke of "a Government with the courage and foresight to permit us to undertake an assignment which has struck the imagination of rural leaders throughout the world."[9]

Or, as Douglas put it more succinctly, "In the ordinary sense it really wasn't a Royal Commission."[10]

Fred Bard

Fred McGuinness wouldn't have believed it if he hadn't seen it for himself. But the "truly impossible," in McGuinness's words, did happen.

During the Easter weekend in 1955, McGuinness, as executive director of Saskatchewan's Golden Jubilee Committee, dropped by to inspect the progress being made on the new Saskatchewan Museum of Natural History. Fred Bard, the museum director, served as his tour guide that day and walked him around the building shell, pointing to recesses where the habitat cases were to go. The problem, though, was that the official opening was a mere two months away, and the walls were still not plastered and wires were hanging down from the ceiling where light fixtures were to go.

McGuinness knew from experience at other museums that Bard and his team of Fred Lahrman and R. D. Symons would be lucky to have one habitat case ready for the opening ceremonies. But on 16 May 1955, when Governor General Vincent Massey officially opened the new building, all of the exhibits had been completed. McGuinness chalked it up to "superhuman efforts." [1]

Frederick George Bard had worked for the Museum of Natural History for more than twenty years before being named director in 1947. Born in Granum, Alberta, in 1908, Fred had quit school at age sixteen

Ornithologist Fred Bard developed the displays for the new Saskatchewan Museum of Natural History, the province's major project for the 1955 diamond jubilee.
SASKATCHEWAN ARCHIVES BOARD R-A5251-1

to apprentice in taxidermy under museum preparator H. H. Mitchell.[2] Bard, an apt and hard-working pupil, grew into the job and became a skilled taxidermist in his own right—so much so that he replaced Mitchell upon his retirement in 1933.

Bard was as much a dedicated field naturalist as a taxidermist and spent several weeks each year collecting museum specimens throughout the province. He also taught himself to make wildlife educational movies of unusual quality. Much of this work was undertaken in the interests of educating the public about Saskatchewan's natural history, a concern underscored by his extensive public speaking on the matter. He once told a Rotary Club meeting that "if they [adults] could promote in young people a real interest in wildlife and natural history—a fascinating subject—they would not have to fear the influence of Elvis Presley and 'Rock and Roll.'"[3]

Bard's specialty was ornithology, in particular the protection of species and habitat. In the 1940s, he became deeply involved in the international campaign to save the majestic whooping crane from possible extinction and was often a spokesperson for their plight. He was also a major player in the Canada Goose Nesting Project, a campaign to reintroduce the over-hunted bird to the prairies. The thousand geese that have now become a nuisance around Wascana Lake and Marsh are testament to the unanticipated effectiveness of Bard's efforts.

When Fred Bard became director of the Museum of Natural History in 1947, the institution was badly in need of a new home. Established in 1906, one year after Saskatchewan entered Confederation as a province, the museum was initially housed in the Regina Trading Company building. It was moved to the Legislative Building in 1911 and then relocated to the Regina Normal School five years later. There, it resided for nearly forty years, except for being temporarily displaced during the Second World War when the building was needed for pilot training.[4]

The big push for a new museum building started in 1944 when the Regina Natural History Society, led by its president, Lloyd Carmichael, petitioned the newly elected CCF government to provide a new, more permanent home for the collection. This campaign picked up momentum following the creation of the Saskatchewan Natural History Society five years later. The new president of the provincial society[5] made a spirited plea for a new building at the annual meeting in the fall of 1952, even sending a letter to Premier Douglas.

But it was a Regina journalist, the formidable Elizabeth Cruickshank, who came up with the winning solution—that the museum honour Saskatchewan pioneers.[6] What a brilliant idea and what perfect timing! With the province's fiftieth birthday only three years away,

Premier Tommy Douglas enthusiastically seized upon this concept and ran with it. "[I]t helped give Saskatchewan people," Douglas later recounted, "an opportunity for thanking the pioneers for what they had done."[7]

In keeping with this spirit and purpose, the new museum was the province's major Jubilee project for 1955. Indeed, the large, elaborate structure, costing one million dollars, far exceeded anyone's dreams. It was also given pride of place. Douglas chose to set the tasteful, beautiful building in the best available position in Regina—Wascana Park at the corner of Albert and College.

The task of preparing the museum displays fell on the shoulders of Bard and his two able assistants. In 1947, the same year he had been promoted to director, Bard hired another young lad, Frederick W. Lahrman, who had been raised on a farm in the hills south of Mortlach. Taught taxidermy by Bard, Lahrman providentially was also a gifted artist. Lahrman painted dozens of world-class background display dioramas, illustrated a number of museum booklets and special publications of the Saskatchewan Natural History Society, and set up the first interpretive displays in Saskatchewan provincial parks.[8]

The second artist, and the third man in this important triumvirate, was the English-born Robert David Symons, a former rancher and game guardian who had been hired by Bard on a commission basis in 1951.[9] Symons spent the long winter months working alongside Lahrman, painting in advance the backdrop paintings for the large displays that became the museum showpieces. These massive canvases were prepared in temporary quarters while the new building was under construction, and were then brought to near-completion in the basement of the new museum building during the winter of 1954–55.

Fred McGuinness, executive director of the Jubilee celebrations, was a regular visitor during the construction of the new museum and expressed amazement at the size of the canvases in the basement. Bard explained to him that he had no desire to equip a standard, static museum, fixed in time and space. He wanted a museum that had a regular flow of repeat patrons who could always find something they had never seen before.[10]

That is exactly what the three men achieved in the breathtaking beauty of the dioramas and habitat displays, each of which showed the mounted animals and birds in a specific Saskatchewan habitat. In some, the three-dimensional effects were so perfect that the foreground of real birds, animals, and vegetation blended into the painted backdrop. The visitor, standing in front of the diorama, had to look carefully. Where exactly did the real birds and cattails end and those of the painted backdrop take over?

The official opening by Governor General Vincent Massey took place in a cold, driving rain that turned the not-yet-landscaped grounds into thick mud.[11] The dedication sculpture, carved in bold relief in Tyndall stone, featured a skyward-looking farmer, clutching sheaves of wheat, along with his wife and female child. The accompanying inscription read:

> THIS MUSEUM OF NATURAL HISTORY IS DEDICATED TO
> THE HONOUR OF ALL THE PIONEERS WHO CAME FROM
> MANY LANDS TO SETTLE IN THIS PART OF CANADA A
> TRIBUTE TO THEIR VISION TOIL AND COURAGE WHICH
> GAVE SO MUCH TO SASKATCHEWAN AND THIS NATION.[12]

Over the next four months, between May and August 1955, 100,900 people visited the new museum. That figure translated into about 11 percent of the Saskatchewan population at the time.[13]

With the new museum building in place, the American Ornithologists' Union accepted an invitation to hold its annual meeting at the museum in late August 1959. It was the first time in the society's history that it had been the guest of a state or provincial government. Premier Douglas hosted the annual banquet, and also supplied the STC buses that took the AOU members on a daytrip to see the unforgettable "spectacle of some 8,000 sandhill cranes" at Canada's oldest bird sanctuary at the north end of Last Mountain Lake.[14] Douglas, in turn, was extremely proud of the AOU enthusiasm for the museum and its staff.

That the plan to build a new Museum of Natural History to honour the province's pioneers had been realized with such great success was in no small part a consequence of Fred Bard's vision and dedication. By the time he retired in 1970, after a forty-five-year career at the museum, he had been named Fellow of the Canadian Museums Association, awarded the Canadian Centennial Medal, and granted an honorary degree. Not bad for a kid who quit school to apprentice as a taxidermist.

Allan Blair

The year 1947 blew into Saskatchewan with a vengeance. Starting in late January, one of the worst blizzards in Canadian history raged across the southern half of the province. A staggering four feet of snow fell in some areas, including the provincial capital, Regina.

At the home of Dr. Allan Blair, director of Saskatchewan Cancer Services for the province, the snow wrapped around two sides of his house on the corner of Hill Avenue and Robinson Street. The drifts even reached the second-floor bedroom windows.

Dr. Blair, with help from family members, decided to carve a tunnel through the snow to the back door of the house. But it was no ordinary excavation. Planning every feature of the operation as if he were preparing for some delicate surgical procedure, Blair first probed the mountain of snow and then prepared a series of maps and diagrams. The completed tunnel was exactly as it had been drawn. After a photograph was taken of Blair, proudly standing in front of his handiwork, he turned to his daughter Pat and said, "Practising good medicine is art applied to science."[1]

Allan Walker Blair was born 28 November 1900, at Brussels, Ontario. He was eleven when his family moved to Regina, where he attended Victoria School and Central Collegiate. Allan did his undergraduate pre-med studies at the University of Saskatchewan, where he played on the varsity football and basketball teams. He also met his future wife, Florence Wilson of Indian Head, who obtained her B.A. in 1923.[2] Blair contracted pneumonia at exam time in the spring of 1923 and did not graduate with his B.Sc. for another year. In a note tucked in the back of his graduation photo, he wrote, "I am now a university graduate but still have three years till I am a medical doctor—the first goal of my dreams ... It remains for me to accomplish something worthwhile."[3]

Blair studied medicine at McGill University and also starred as the quarterback for the Redmen football team.[4] One summer, he worked as a porter for the Canadian Pacific Railway. His turnaround in Regina gave him a chance to visit with family and continue courting Florence.

Blair studied medicine at McGill University and also starred as quarterback for the Redmen football team. PAT KRAUSE

The pair were married at the end of June 1928 in her hometown and, after a short honeymoon in Fort Qu'Appelle, left for Montreal on separate trains. "Hardest three nights I spent as a porter," Blair later recalled.[5]

Upon completing his internship in 1928, Blair taught pathology at McGill for a year before moving on to the University of Alabama School of Medicine in Tuscaloosa. There, he created headlines in November 1933 when he allowed a black widow spider to bite him in order to learn first-hand about the effect of the venom on the human body. The experiment landed him in hospital in excruciating pain for three days.

In the early 1930s, Blair spent three summers back at

McGill, studying anaesthesia, medicine, and surgery, respectively.[6] He was tired of practising pathology at Tuscaloosa and, at the first opportunity, he returned to Canada in 1934 to become senior resident in surgery at Winnipeg's General Hospital. But he continued his cancer training.

In 1935–36, as the first Canadian ever awarded a Rockefeller Fellowship, Blair worked at the New York Memorial Hospital for Cancer and Allied Diseases and attended radiation lectures given by the famous physicist Edith Quimby. The following year, he boarded a freighter for Europe and spent nine months doing post-graduate study in Edinburgh, and then visiting eight of the leading European cancer centres (Manchester, London, Paris, Brussels, Louvain, Frankfurt, Hamburg, and Stockholm).[7]

On completion of these studies, Blair was named associate director of the Toronto Institute of Radiology. But that only lasted for eighteen months. In the spring of 1939 he was enticed back to Saskatchewan to take charge of the Regina Cancer Clinic. Blair wired his pal, Dr. Joe Brown, an obstetrician in Regina, for advice. Brown's response, also by telegram, consisted of six words, "You will be your own boss."[8] That was sufficient encouragement. Blair accepted the job.

Allan Blair was specifically recruited to reinvigorate and promote cancer treatment in Saskatchewan. In 1930, the Anderson government had set a North American precedent with the passage of the Saskatchewan Cancer Commission Act. Two government-sponsored, part-time (two mornings a week) cancer clinics—one in Regina General Hospital, the other at Saskatoon City Hospital—were established to provide consultation, diagnosis, and radiation therapy. It was a groundbreaking initiative in cancer treatment, as reflected in the growing number of patients referred each year to the two clinics.[9]

But these services did not come free. The hospital clinics were empowered to collect fees from patients, or, in the case of the poor, secure payment for indigent cases from their home municipalities. This proved to be a serious problem during the Great Depression. As of 1935, it was estimated that almost half the cancer inpatients at the two

Allan Blair served as director of cancer services in Saskatchewan during the early years of the Douglas government. SASKATCHEWAN ARCHIVES BOARD R-B11015

hospital clinics could not pay for their treatment.[10] The financial burden consequently fell on municipalities, which were already struggling to provide relief assistance during the 1930s.

The funding shortfall came to a head in 1939. Regina General

Hospital requested payment from the provincial cancer commission to cover a ballooning cancer clinic deficit. When the commission refused, the hospital reported that it could no longer afford to treat indigent cases without payment. This stalemate prompted the commission to find a new home for the Regina clinic, Grey Nun's Hospital.[11] The commission also decided that the cancer program needed new leadership.

Into this difficult situation stepped Allan Blair. The thirty-eight-year-old cancer specialist was hired by the commission as supervising therapist and head of the new Regina clinic, with a mandate to breathe new life into the province's cancer program. He was up to the task.

Dr. Blair's training was the equal of almost any radiotherapist in North America, certainly in Canada, at the time. He was also intent on providing quality treatment and care. His motto for the Regina cancer clinic, according to his daughter Pat, was: "Errors of omission are inexcusable … Errors of commission are regarded with tolerance and understanding."[12] What really kept him going, though, in his battle to eradicate cancer was his irrepressible love of life. "His wit was delightful," commented one newspaper story, "the twinkle in his eye constant."[13]

Blair worked tirelessly over the next few years to increase the number of patients being seen at the province's two cancer clinics, while pushing for a corresponding increase in the size of the medical staff. The real turning point, though, came in the fall of 1944 when the new Tommy Douglas government introduced cancer control legislation as one of its first measures. The act signalled that cancer was not only a serious disease, but that its diagnosis and treatment were often beyond the means of Saskatchewan citizens. These services were now to be provided free of charge under the new Cancer Control Act.

Dr. Blair was at the centre of this renewed provincial campaign against cancer in his capacity as the new director of cancer services for Saskatchewan. He also spearheaded the formation of the National Cancer Institute in 1947 and served as its first president.[14] Premier Douglas personally placed great faith in Blair and readily supported his requests for grants to send clinic doctors, nurses, and technicians away to get specialized training at leading cancer treatment facilities.

The CCF premier also appreciated Blair's foresight in pursuing the newest advances in cancer radiation technology for use in the province. It's unfortunate that Blair did not live long enough to see the results of his efforts.

Allan Blair died in early November 1948, a few weeks shy of his forty-eighth birthday, and only five months after the opening of the cancer clinic he had helped design. It was not cancer that felled him, but a fatal heart attack.

An editorial in the *Regina Leader-Post* described Blair as a great healer, while a deeply saddened Douglas spoke of "Saskatchewan … suffer[ing] an irreparable loss."[15] The premier even suggested that his workload on behalf of the province's cancer victims had hastened his death. "If ever a man lay down his life in the service of humanity," Douglas observed, "it was Dr. Allan Blair."[16] That unselfish service was recognized in the naming of the new Regina cancer clinic building in his memory.[17]

Brandon College Teachers

———————————— ✂ ————————————

It was Tommy Douglas's first job in the ministry—a supply preacher in a small country church outside Winnipeg in the summer of 1922. When he arrived at the Stonewall station that Sunday morning, there was a large crowd, scanning the passengers as they got off the train. The diminutive Tommy slipped through the people, walked up to a local boy leaning against his bicycle, and asked directions to the Baptist church, saying he was there to give the service. The incredulous boy shouted down the platform: "Mom, this kid says he's the new preacher!"[1]

Tommy could see the immediate disappointment on the faces of the congregation. But when he finished the service, they happily invited the preacher with the boyish looks back the following Sunday.

In 1922, Tommy Douglas, an apprentice printer, decided to devote his life to Christian service and enter the ministry.[2] Although his parents had never interfered in his choice of careers, his mother, Anne, was extremely pleased. "She told me," Tommy remembered, "that this was what she had always hoped I would do." He felt much the same way. "The general feeling," he admitted, "was that if I had any useful contribution to make at all it was probably in the Christian church."[3] Many who knew him suggested that he should try his hand at something

Tommy Douglas graduation photo, Brandon College Academy. BRANDON UNIVERSITY ARCHIVES

that would make greater use of his speaking skills.

In retrospect, becoming a minister was a logical step for the eighteen-year-old. Tommy had joined the Baptist church when he came to Canada and since then had always been involved in church activities. In particular, he greatly enjoyed the fellowship of the young people's meetings and wanted the opportunity to work with young boys and try to make a difference in their lives. The church seemed to be the answer. Or at least, it was calling him. His minister at Beulah Baptist Church would sometimes ask him to take over the Sunday evening service. He found that he liked preaching, that he liked church work in general. It was a way, he had come to believe after witnessing the turmoil of post-war Winnipeg, to help bring about a better world.

To get to college, Tommy first had to find the money. He spent a year saving whatever did not go toward supporting the family household; he could not count on his parents' financial support and did not want to. He also borrowed books from his friends and spent time reading and studying in preparation for his classes. Tommy had been out of school for four years and wanted to be ready when he finally resumed his education. More important, though, was finding another source of income, since he would be giving up his job in the printing business. Here, Tommy was personally helped by the Manitoba Superintendent of Missions, who found the aspiring minister work as a supply preacher.

Tommy entered Brandon College, "a combination liberal arts and missionary training school founded by the Baptist Church,"[4] in

September 1924. He was one month shy of his twentieth birthday. He would spend six years there, completing his high school requirements (his senior matriculation) and then his theology training as part of his Bachelor of Arts degree.

These were difficult days for organized religion in Canada. In 1925, members of the Methodist and Congregational churches, along with most Presbyterian congregations, came together to form the United Church of Canada. The new church placed less emphasis on personal salvation and the afterlife in favour of applying the teachings of Christ to everyday social problems—what was known as the "social gospel." The goal was to bring about the "Kingdom of God on Earth." Some Protestant denominations, however, continued to support a more traditional or literal interpretation of the Bible, and heaped scorn on the social gospel enthusiasts.

These tensions were played out within the walls of Brandon College, as faculty and students argued over the meaning and interpretation of the Scriptures. Indeed, three teachers who did not shy away from the controversy played especially important roles in the education of Tommy Douglas.

First, and most important, was Harris Lachlan MacNeill, Tommy's professor of New Testament, Latin, and Greek, and one of the most controversial instructors at Brandon.[5] MacNeill

Harris Lachlan MacNeill was described by Douglas as one of the forces that shaped "his social philosophy."
CANADIAN BAPTIST ARCHIVES, MCMASTER DIVINITY COLLEGE

was a modernist who openly challenged the fundamentalists and their deep-seated convictions. Two years before Tommy's arrival at Brandon, a special church commission had investigated MacNeill for heresy, but acquitted the teacher in the end.[6]

MacNeill gave the Gospel, in Tommy's words, "a new meaning; rather than an earthly kingdom based on power and might and on the sword, it was to be a Kingdom of the spirit in men's hearts, made up of righteousness and justice." Some students found this liberal thinking too radical, while others admired it and the conviction with which it was voiced. Tommy was one of those he won over. "It liberalized my views," he confessed.[7]

Tommy quickly came to admire MacNeill and what he stood for. He once described him as "a giant among pygmies." He also credited MacNeill for being one of the forces that shaped "his social philosophy." Tommy even went so far as to suggest that he was responsible for "any intellectual curiosity I have."[8]

Tommy's second Brandon College mentor was Alfred E. Johns, his professor of mathematics and a former Baptist missionary in Chengtu,[9] West China.

The Johns family regularly invited Douglas home for Sunday dinner. SUGARING OFF

More than fifty years later, Douglas fondly remembered how Johns had taken a special interest in the young theological student because he was "both poor and undernourished." He recalled, "The osteomyelitis in my femur was chronic, would periodically break down and issue pus, and this ran me down. The Johns family took pity on me, and often had me over for Sunday supper, in a deliberate attempt to put some weight on my frame."[10] Douglas would forever appreciate the generosity.

The third teacher was Dr. J. R. C. Evans, professor of science but particularly geology, who became president of Brandon College in 1928. Evans fully appreciated that "it is not always easy [at the college] to bring the denominational point of view and the academic view together."[11] But he actively encouraged scientific inquiry, even at the expense of challenging his own Christian convictions.

Popularly known to students as "the Doc," Evans taught Douglas the value of a scientific approach to problems—in other words, "the ability to identify and ask the right questions, to grasp the essence of a matter rather than its superficial characteristics."[12] These skills would become a hallmark of the Douglas style.

Evans also served as coach for Douglas and the Brandon debating team. "I still follow his system in laying out a speech," Tommy once explained. "He had a scientific approach. He didn't just get into a subject and wallow around."[13] Tommy got the opportunity to put this

Popularly known to students as "the Doc," Professor J. R. C. Evans taught Douglas the value of a scientific approach to problems.
BRANDON UNIVERSITY ARCHIVES

training into practice when Dr. Evans arranged for him and fellow student Stanley Knowles to preach at Weyburn's Calvary Baptist Church on alternate Sundays through the winter of 1929–30.

Tommy Douglas graduated from Brandon College in June 1930 as the Great Depression descended on Canada. The record-low commodity prices, coupled with the long and persistent drought, severely tested his faith in what the church could achieve. He could see that his Weyburn congregation was doing everything humanly possible to alleviate the suffering caused by the Depression but making little headway.

Douglas personally responded to the crisis by drawing on what the trio of Brandon teachers had instilled in him—the freedom of thought, the questioning of orthodoxy, and the search for answers. It wasn't long before he abandoned the pulpit and took up socialist politics.

Bill Burak

It was a manoeuvre that took even the forward-looking Tommy Douglas by surprise. In November 1945, Bill Burak, secretary-treasurer of the Rural Municipality (RM) of Pittville, forced the new CCF government not only to name the Swift Current area as the demonstration health unit for the province but also to allow the region to offer a full suite of medical services.

Premier Douglas certainly planned to go in this direction, but was worried about failing, especially if the provincial government moved too hastily. He consequently wanted any new experimental health region, wherever it was located in the province, to offer preventive services only. But Douglas, as others had learned, "did not reckon on Bill Burak."[1] With fortuitous timing, Burak effectively did an end run—admittedly in the guise of a friendly amendment—on the Douglas government and helped initiate the first medicare scheme in North America. It was years ahead of the planned timetable.

William James Burak was born into poverty on 1 April 1905. His father, Jakim Burak, fresh from Ukraine, had applied for a homestead in the Hirzel (later Goodeve) district of Saskatchewan, along the southern edge of the Beaver Hills, in 1903. The wet and bushy land was never meant for cultivation—even though Jakim managed to clear

Bill Burak was the instigator and driving force behind the creation of the Swift Current experimental health region, where a full range of health services was offered to more than fifty thousand people. SASKATCHEWAN ARCHIVES BOARD R-B7128

twenty acres when not working as a labourer—and the farm soon
failed. The Burak family, with two young children, thereafter eked
out an existence in Goodeve, raising cows, chickens, and bees. This
meagre income was supplemented by a contract with the post office,
which required Jakim to meet the 1 A.M. and 4 A.M. Grand Trunk Pacific trains and retrieve the mail and any parcels.

At sixteen, Bill was sent to high school in Saskatoon at the Ukrai-
nian-based Mohyla Institute. He then trained as a teacher, and after
graduating from the Saskatoon Normal School in 1925, taught for
seventeen years at a number of rural and village schools.[2] This experience in the classroom, together with his hardscrabble upbringing, prepared him to play a pivotal role in the eventual attainment of medicare
in Saskatchewan.

In January 1943, Bill Burak was appointed secretary-treasurer of the
RM of Pittville, centred on the then-unregistered hamlet of Hazlet
on the eastern edge of the arid and barren Great Sand Hills. The region, in the southwest corner of the province, had been brought to its
knees by the Great Depression of the 1930s. The double whammy of
low commodity prices and prolonged drought had precipitated a great
out-migration as farm families chose to start over to the north or left
the province entirely. Those people who remained behind watched
helplessly as "the prairies burned—the skies shed not a tear."[3]

These conditions undermined the provision of basic services, including health care. A survey at the end of the Second World War
found only eighteen doctors in the region—or one for every 3,050
residents.[4] Health care facilities, meanwhile, were inadequate and outdated. The isolation only exacerbated the situation. So, too, did the
distance that people had to travel for treatment.

The RM of Pittville began to address these problems in 1937 by
co-operating with the neighbouring RM to the north (Riverside) and
paying part of the salary of a municipal doctor.[5] But when that doctor enlisted in the Canadian Army in 1941, Pittville took even more
dramatic action by using the RM health tax, already in place, to pay
for their residents to go to "any physician anywhere ... any surgeon

in Canada … stay at any hospital in Canada."[6] This arrangement was unprecedented, if not contrary to the Municipal Act, in that RMs were supposed to strike prior contracts with doctors and hospitals. In fact, one of Burak's first tasks as Pittville secretary-treasurer was to go to Regina in April 1943 and justify this comprehensive but open-ended health plan.[7]

Burak quickly became the scheme's greatest promoter. When the new CCF government hired Dr. Henry Sigerist of Johns Hopkins University to conduct a survey of provincial health services in September 1944, Burak presented a detailed brief, full of impressive facts and statistics. He extolled the merits of the unorthodox Pittville system, noting how it was "very well-liked by the people"[8] and by the serving doctors and hospitals (because they could count on getting paid). Most Pittville mothers, for example, were now able to have their babies delivered in hospital.[9]

Sigerist undoubtedly liked what he heard from Burak, for he, too, believed that the Saskatchewan government should eventually introduce a comprehensive medical insurance plan. But where the two men differed was the timing. In his report to the CCF government, Sigerist recommended that the introduction of medicare should be a gradual development—a strategy supported by Tommy Douglas. All the Saskatchewan premier was prepared to do in the fall of 1944 was create one experimental health region to offer preventive services only.

That was all the opening that the whirlwind Burak needed.[10] In January 1945, he wrote every municipality in the southwest, proposing that they come together to form a health region to offer not just preventive medicine but a full health plan. Nothing more came of the matter, though, until August, when provincial officials came to Swift Current to talk to civic and rural representatives about a new hospital for the region. Burak was there on behalf of Pittville and once again urged his colleagues to think bigger: Swift Current should become a regional health centre and draw on the provincial funding that came with such a designation. Several representatives insisted that the hospital situation was a more pressing matter. But in the end, Burak was appointed a committee of one to canvass the adjacent municipalities about his scheme.

Over the next few weeks, at his own expense, never reimbursed, Burak mailed out two mimeographed circular letters and visited weekly newspapers and municipal councils. He also convinced several RMs, starting with his own, to petition the provincial government to name Swift Current as the new demonstration health region. He capped this effort with a large informational meeting in Swift Current on 15 September 1945, at which representatives from forty-one RMs talked about what services the health region would offer and how they would be funded.

Faced with this groundswell of support for the Burak plan, the provincial government put the matter to a vote. Douglas went on the radio and said that any new health region should initially concentrate on public health services. Burak countered in a series of short articles in regional weeklies, arguing that the new regional health board would decide what services would be offered and that complete health services might cost only ten dollars per person.

On 26 November 1945, residents of the southwest voted 71 percent in favour of Burak's plan.[11] The Douglas government, by order-in-council, acceded to this "fast-tracking" of universal hospital and medical care for the region. Swift Current Health Region #1 came into force on 1 July 1946, two full years in advance of Great Britain's much-better-known National Health Insurance Plan.[12]

Bill Burak wanted to be secretary-treasurer of the new health region. But at an organizational meeting at Gull Lake on 17 January 1946, his candidacy for the position was not even considered. The RM of Pittville responded to Burak's shabby treatment by sending an angry letter of protest to the incipient regional board: "We hope that there was no thought of racial discrimination ... [he] devoted more time to it than any other person ... Swift Current region was organized not as a result of government initiative but as a result of Mr. Burak's initiative and his determination."[13]

It was a crushing disappointment. Burak moved out of the area entirely and held municipal positions at Ogema, Hafford, and finally, Aberdeen. He wrote two books, *Our Ancestors,* a history of Ukraine prior to 1000 A.D.,[14] and a *Ukrainian Phonetic Dictionary.* He died in Saskatoon on 8 June 1976.

The community history book for the Miry Creek RM remembers Bill Burak as "a mover and a shaker."[15] What motivated him was a dream he shared with Tommy Douglas—to bring quality, affordable health care to Saskatchewan's population regardless of ability to pay. Burak just wanted to realize the dream a little faster.

George Cadbury

He was reportedly the power behind the throne—or in this case, the power behind the man who was running Saskatchewan.

During a raucous 1948 provincial election debate in Yorkton, Walter Tucker, the new leader of the provincial Liberal party, came out swinging against Premier Tommy Douglas and his record over the past four years in power. Playing upon Cold War fears and the threat posed by Soviet Russia, Tucker charged that the Reds were behind the CCF government, even secretly funding it. He also accused government planners, recruited from outside the province, of wishing to turn Saskatchewan into a police state.

The person who was directing this wholesale makeover of the province, according to Tucker, was not Douglas, but actually George Cadbury, chairman of the Economic Advisory and Planning Board (EAPB).

Tucker was right in one respect. George Woodall Cadbury was handling a big job on behalf of the Saskatchewan government.

When the CCF was elected in 1944, some members of the new government interpreted their electoral mandate as an order to "get things done."[1] No cabinet minister better represented this gung-ho attitude than Joe Phelps, who handled the Natural Resources portfolio. Phelps vowed to secure complete government ownership of

British-born socialist George Cadbury served as head of the powerful Economic Advisory and Planning Board. SASKATCHEWAN ARCHIVES BOARD R-A112191-1

the province's key industries and then went on a shopping spree. He bought a Regina shoe factory/tannery, Moose Jaw woollen mill, and Prince Albert box factory—with little or no consultation. When the cabinet, after a prolonged debate, voted against the purchase of a defunct brick plant in Estevan, the Natural Resources minister exclaimed, "But by gosh fellows. I've already bought it." [2]

Phelps believed, naively, that these enterprises would wean the province from its over-dependence on agriculture and help bring about a more diversified economy for the benefit of all citizens. But the new manufacturing ventures were undertaken without much analysis, and they soon began to lose money, largely because of the small Saskatchewan market and the availability of cheaper out-of-province imports. Their eventual closure not only demonstrated the potential perils of public ownership, but also served as a source of embarrassment to the government for years to come.

Tommy Douglas was not pleased. He had always talked about the value of government planning, but Phelps's activities were undermining the CCF's credibility. According to one observer, the government's first few years in office were nothing short of "chaotic ... the root causes ... related to poor planning, a shortage of trained managers, and an ignorance of management methods." [3]

To help clean up this mess, Premier Douglas hired George Cadbury, a British Fabian socialist of the chocolate family fame, to advise the cabinet on how best to direct future economic policy "in the interests of the population with a view to ... the economic and social problems with which the government had to deal." [4]

But his appointment as head of the new Economic Advisory and Planning Board elicited a stern rebuke from the Opposition, which maintained that such practices were foreign to Saskatchewan. The Liberal leader even suggested in a Regina radio broadcast that control of the government had passed to "a shadowy group." [5]

George Cadbury arrived in Regina to start his new job for the CCF government on a January day in early 1946. Despite the weather, he was happy to get off the train. His six-foot-five-inch frame was not meant for a sleeping berth. The next morning—after sleeping diagonally across two beds in the Hotel Saskatchewan—he told a reporter for *Time* magazine that "socialism in all of Canada is inevitable" and that he looked upon Regina as "a city of opportunity."[6]

Cadbury's recruitment was nothing less than a coup for the Douglas government—not only because of his business credentials, but his political leanings. Al Johnson, another public servant at the time, called the move "a singularly important step."[7]

Born in Birmingham on 19 January 1907, Cadbury was the eldest grandchild (although son of the third son) of the Quaker founder of the famous chocolate dynasty. In the 1920s he attended King's College at Cambridge University, where John Maynard Keynes was his supervisor in economics. He later studied at the Wharton School of Business at the University of Pennsylvania. He had been director of a co-operative cannery and a custard powder firm in Britain, separate from the family's chocolate business. During the Second World War, he was deputy director of aircraft production in Great Britain for three years. He had close ties with the British Labour Party.

Cadbury essentially served as "the premier's right-hand man."[8] The pair could easily have been mistaken for Saskatchewan's version of the comedic duo, Mutt and Jeff. The folksy Douglas was dwarfed by the handsome, sophisticated Cadbury, "imposing in his intelligence and his reasoning."[9] But they both shared a vision of what a social democratic government could achieve. In particular, "Cadbury was an administratively competent professional economist, ideologically committed to an active entrepreneurial state, imbued with a respect for British parliamentary practice and the rightful supremacy of cabinet within that system. He was also a shrewd bureaucrat who avoided sharp head-on conflicts with his nominal superiors in cabinet."[10]

In his first major report to Cabinet in the fall of 1946, Cadbury proposed a mixed economy for the province. The Saskatchewan government should still strive to create new businesses, but in areas that offered greater promise of success, such as non-agricultural staples. He also argued that government's economic blueprint should include the active encouragement of private investment. This EAPB recommendation was clearly at odds with the founding philosophy of the party, but it reflected the reality of the situation—and the reality of staying in power for the CCF, which had already moved miles beyond its 1930s beginnings. In short, the report was "a needed lesson in common sense."[11]

The EAPB under Cadbury spawned two other innovative structures: in November 1946, the Budget Bureau (BB), and in 1947, the Government Finance Office (GFO, later the Crown Investments Corporation). These initiatives went a long way in providing the kind of long range, integrated economic planning that Douglas had advocated. *Time* magazine certainly seemed impressed. Returning to Saskatchewan to do a follow-up story on the province's "imported British socialist," the journalist reported that "Saskatchewan's pinks had done a good job of keeping Saskatchewan out of the red."[12]

With things running smoothly, and because he enjoyed building, not administering, Cadbury felt that the creative part of his task had been completed, and he left early in 1951. He spent the next nine years with the United Nations as director of Technical Assistance.

Upon retirement in 1960, Cadbury settled in Ontario, where he served as president of the provincial NDP. With his wife, Barbara, he also helped found what would become the Planned Parenthood Federation of Canada. Their successful campaign to have contraception removed from Canada's criminal code in 1969 earned the couple the Order of Canada in 1990. Cadbury died five years later in Oakville at age eighty-eight.

Interestingly, obituaries focused on his birth control work and paid scant attention to his years in Saskatchewan. It was as if the public servant once accused of being in charge of the province had played an anonymous role.

Irma Dempsey

———————————— ✖ ————————————

Tommy Douglas had a well-earned reputation as a scrapper—a trait
he acquired during his amateur boxing days in Winnipeg. He delighted in the thrust and parry of public debate, whether on the campaign
hustings or in the Saskatchewan Legislature, and was rarely bested by
his opponents, who always seemed lacklustre by comparison. But during his senior year at Brandon College, Tommy and his debating team
went down to an ignoble defeat by a stunning unanimous decision.
The opposing team featured Irma Dempsey, a bright young woman
with an infectious laugh. "It is difficult to believe that even given the
chance, he would have deliberately thrown the debate," reasoned one
of Tommy's friends. "It seems more likely that he had, in fact, at last
met his match."[1]

Once twenty-year-old Tommy Douglas enrolled in Brandon College
in 1924, he had to find a way to support himself. Fortunately, even
during his three high school years at the college academy, he was offered the prospect of supply preaching in rural churches, usually ones
that could be reached by train. For this service, student preachers
earned eight dollars per Sunday during the academic year and fifteen
dollars a week in the summer months.

The Douglas-Dempsey wedding on 30 August 1930 (left to right: Nellie Dempsey, Hull Dempsey, Dean Dempsey, Irma Dempsey, and T. C. Douglas). CARBERRY PLAINS MUSEUM

Tommy not only embraced these assignments—and the experience they provided—but was something of a pioneer in ecumenism.[2] Although Brandon College turned out Baptist ministers, he readily agreed in 1925 to fill the vacant *Free Presbyterian* pulpit at Carberry, only twenty-eight miles east along the CPR line to Winnipeg.[3] It quickly turned into a regular posting for the next two years.

One of the local teens who switched churches to hear the "boy preacher" was Irma Dempsey, the daughter of a local farmer and a Methodist by upbringing. The Dempseys, refugees from the great Irish potato famine, had initially settled in the Ottawa Valley before homesteading in Manitoba in the early twentieth century.

Irma, described as "petite, brown-haired … with shining eyes,"[4] quickly became a fixture in the Presbyterian congregation and looked forward to Tommy's weekly visits to Carberry. The growing friendship between the pair may have influenced her decision to study piano at Brandon College following her graduation from high school in 1928.

There, the relationship became more serious under the watchful eye of Mrs. Dempsey, who had accompanied her daughter to Brandon as chaperone.

But what secured the family's blessing, according to Tommy, was his knowledge of horses. Irma's father, Hull Dempsey, was a horse dealer, locally renowned for the quality of his stock. Douglas, on the other hand, had sometimes looked after his Grandfather Clement's horses in Scotland. He had also helped clean the harnesses for a team of Clydes. "If I hadn't been able to talk to Irma's dad about horses," he half-jokingly recounted, "I doubt that he would have ever let me marry his daughter."[5]

Tommy and Irma were married on Saturday, 30 August 1930, exactly two months to the day from his graduation. Tommy's brother-in-law, Mark Talnicoff, a Baptist minister at Portage la Prairie, performed the service, while Tommy's Brandon College classmate, Stanley Knowles, stood up as his best man. The morning after the wedding, and the Sunday following, Tommy preached in Stanley Knowles's church in Winnipeg, while Knowles preached both Sundays in Tommy's church in Weyburn.[6] Short of money, Tommy and Irma spent their honeymoon in his parents' home in Winnipeg, the only free accommodation available.

This supply preaching to make ends meet had become common practice for Douglas. In fact, it enabled him to complete his schooling at Brandon. But what about his young bride? "Of course they used to warn the girls at college to stay away from the theologs," Tommy remembered, "or they'd end up in a drafty manse somewhere, getting their clothes out of a missionary box."[7] Irma, however, had no such worries and looked forward to her new life in Weyburn as the wife of the new minister at Calvary Baptist Church.

She could not have asked for a better welcome. When the newly married couple arrived at the Weyburn train station that September, they were warmly greeted by the Calvary Baptist congregation and a "brass band, which serenaded them all the way to their first residence, an apartment above a downtown store."[8] For Irma, barely nineteen, it

Tommy's brother-in-law Mark Talnicoff performed the marriage ceremony (left to right: Mark Talnicoff, Nan (Douglas) Talnicoff, T. C. Douglas, and Irma Dempsey). CARBERRY PLAINS MUSEUM

was her first trip outside Manitoba. Her husband, soon to be twenty-six, had a princely $5.39 in his pocket.

These would be challenging days for Tommy and Irma. Douglas had assumed the ministry at Calvary Baptist at the worst possible time. Not only had the Saskatchewan economy been rocked by the Great Depression, but Weyburn was in the heart of the dust bowl. The church would be on the front lines in trying to deal with the ever-worsening crisis.

Irma, as the minister's wife, pitched in wherever and whenever she could without a word of complaint. "The phone never stopped and you would never know if you would have two people for a meal or whether you would have four or more. You're young, you know, and you don't know if you get tired."[9] Irma played the piano in church and during Tommy's regular visits to the local mental hospital. She also contributed to a sewing circle, established by her husband, which provided clothes to the needy. And she became a regular customer of a hard-working farmer and member of the Baptist congregation, who had been reduced to peddling butter, cream, eggs, and plucked chickens and turkeys door-to-door in Weyburn.

"Irma accepted the town, the job, and the challenge with an equanimity that seldom left her," noted one author. "The church, as is so often the case, got two workers for one salary."[10]

Irma's unflinching support and devotion became even more important once Tommy was elected to the House of Commons in 1935. She largely shouldered the responsibility for raising their two daughters, Shirley and Joan, and running their Weyburn home while Tommy attended to his MP duties in Ottawa. "She organized everything," noted Joan. "I'm sure she could have run General Motors."[11]

These absences would not be as long once Tommy returned to Saskatchewan to lead the CCF Party to victory in the 1944 provincial election. About three months later, the Douglas family moved into their Regina home at 217 Angus Crescent. Under a headline: "Domestic arts to the fore: Premier's wife lends help from fireside," the *Regina Leader-Post* reported that Mrs. Douglas was completing a pair of ribbed green and red socks. "My husband won't wear any other kind of socks but the ones I make so I have to keep him supplied." She explained that she was "really a domestic-minded soul who had always done her own housework and who enjoyed cooking, preserving and such ... Despite the din generated by decorators busy in the kitchen and frequent interruptions by telephone and doorbell, Mrs. Douglas never appeared ruffled."[12]

But the demands on Tommy's time—now that he was premier—were even greater, and they enjoyed little family time together, away from the worries of running the government, except during their annual vacations at Carlyle Lake.[13] He admitted to a reporter in 1958 that "the number of meals I have at home are pretty limited ... I'll be lucky to get three meals a week at home."[14]

There also continued to be money worries. In 1948, when Opposition Leader Walter Tucker filed a slander and libel suit against Douglas for one hundred thousand dollars, Irma nervously met Tommy at the door and said, "Where in heaven's name are we going to get a hundred thousand dollars?" Even though her husband eventually won the case, the legal fees kept them "broke for quite a while."[15]

But the pair never let the demands of Tommy's job or other worries intrude on their happiness together. "There were always jokes and laughter," remembered long-time friend Irene Spry. "Tommy and Irma had a quality of direct friendliness and simplicity about them … there was never the slightest trace of pomposity in either Tommy or Irma."[16] That included Irma sneaking some sandwiches and chocolate bars in the cuff of her fur coat into the June 1953 Westminster Abbey coronation of Queen Elizabeth II.[17]

Irma's most important duty, though, was to her husband and providing a sanctuary during his years as Saskatchewan premier. When Tommy arrived home from the Legislature, she instinctively took the telephone off the hook before she served supper. The two Douglas daughters never forgot what their mom did for their dad. "Mom built him not only a castle, but almost a fortress," Joan recounted.[18] "Nothing was allowed to disturb him at home." Shirley added, "There was something about the atmosphere—it was the coolest, quietest, calmest house I've ever been in."[19]

During her fifty-six years of married life with Tommy, Irma was very much in the background. She wanted it that way. But there was no denying what her companionship meant to Tommy, even if it was something as simple as a late evening walk together around the block.

When Tommy retired from the House of Commons in 1979, his BC riding honoured the Douglas couple with a testimonial dinner. Tommy talked about the importance of having Irma at his side during his lengthy, at times stormy, political career: "Irma was always there with a cheerful word, no matter how black things were, no matter how dark it was, no matter how many lickings we'd taken," he lovingly said. "The darker it got the more cheerful she was."[20]

Sylvia Fedoruk

It was the first and only time that Sylvia Fedoruk met Saskatchewan Premier Tommy Douglas. In early March 1961, the Joyce McKee rink, with Fedoruk playing third, won the first-ever Canadian women's curling title (forerunner of the Scotties Tournament of Hearts). The women were honoured later that spring at the Saskatchewan Legislature, with the premier acting more like a cheerleader.

Little did Douglas realize, though, that Fedoruk was more than a skilled curler. Ten years earlier, she brought the same precision to her work as a young graduate student in physics at the University of Saskatchewan and accurately calibrated the famous "cobalt bomb" that revolutionized cancer treatment in the province and around the world.

Sylvia Olga Fedoruk was born at Canora, Saskatchewan, on 5 May 1927. Her father was a teacher in one-room schools in rural Saskatchewan, but during the Second World War, he moved the family to Windsor, Ontario, so that he could do factory war work. Sylvia was the top female graduate in her high school and returned west to pursue her undergraduate degree at the University of Saskatchewan. She not only continued to excel in her studies, but on the playing field as well. Sylvia was a member of twelve university championship teams (basketball, track and field, golf, volleyball, and hockey). She was also

As a University of Saskatchewan student, Sylvia Fedoruk was a member of twelve championship teams (basketball, track and field, golf, volleyball, and hockey).
UNIVERSITY OF SASKATCHEWAN ARCHIVES A6236

a gifted softball player. Her later success on the curling rink was really no surprise.[1]

Sylvia graduated with a B.A. in 1949, pocketing the Governor-

General's Medal "as the most distinguished graduate of any college."[2] She also won the "Spirit of Youth" award for her many achievements, including her involvement in student governance. Given Sylvia's various talents, she probably could have done anything. Still, it was unusual that she chose the physical sciences, a field largely restricted to men at the time.

Sylvia began work in the master's program in physics, under the supervision of Harold Johns, in the fall of 1950. Fedoruk was Johns's first female graduate student. That was significant in itself. But Johns also held a joint appointment with the Saskatchewan Cancer Commission and was in search of a more effective and less expensive form of radiation therapy.

When Fedoruk entered the graduate program, the Physics Department was already home to a betatron, a new high-energy radiation source that was being used by the Saskatoon cancer clinic as of March 1949. When Saskatchewan had decided to secure a betatron in 1946, Dr. Allan Blair, director of cancer services for the province, had insisted, "It is not planned to use it for any actual treatment until the physical measurements have been completed to everyone's satisfaction."[3] This pre-condition, the cornerstone of all future Saskatchewan research in radiation therapy, meant that the betatron, once installed, was not operational for nine months to allow for the development and completion of radiation depth-dose charts.

The betatron treatment costs, though, were prohibitive, prompting Johns to try to harness the powerful radiation emitted by the new isotope, cobalt-60. Some questioned whether cobalt-60 could be used for this therapeutic purpose, while others believed that this pioneering cancer research would best be carried out in one of Canada's larger centres—certainly not Saskatoon. Fedoruk consequently found herself, at age twenty-three, at the controversial forefront of radiation science.

Johns took delivery of his radioactive cobalt source on 30 July 1951. He had waited almost two years for the Chalk River nuclear plant to "cook" what Johns's wife casually described as "a little half-inch stack

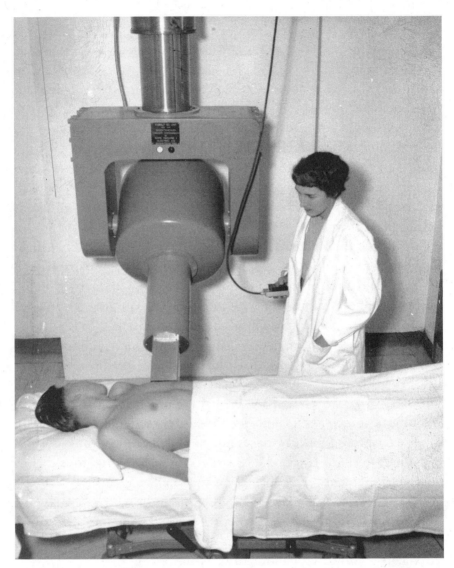

Sylvia Fedoruk's job, and the subject of her master's thesis, was to prepare the rigorous depth-dose measurements for the new cobalt-60 cancer treatment unit at the university hospital.
SASKATCHEWAN CANCER AGENCY

of these cobalt discs about the size of a quarter." [4] It was a real coup for Saskatoon and the university, but there was still much more to be done before the cobalt-60 was ready.

First, Johns had to devise a machine to safely hold the cobalt-60. He also had to find a way to administer the correct dosage; otherwise, given the strength of cobalt-60, the patient could easily be exposed to too much radiation. These requirements could not be hurried. But Johns and his University of Saskatchewan team were not the only group in Canada at work on cobalt-60. The federal crown corporation, Eldorado Mining and Refining, was racing to develop a second cobalt-60 facility, which they placed in London's Victoria Hospital.[5]

Johns designed the Saskatoon unit with one of his other graduate students, Lloyd Bates. They decided to mount the radioactive source on the circumference of a wheel near the centre of the head. By rotating the wheel, the source could be moved 180 degrees from its shielded resting position until it was opposite an opening or exit port through which the radiation emerged.

The half-ton unit, built by local machinist Johnny MacKay of Acme Machine and Electric in Saskatoon, was installed in Room 167 in the newly constructed cancer wing of University Hospital on 17 August 1951. The room was hardly ready for use; the thick walls were still being plastered, while the concrete floor had yet to be poured. Johns, however, went ahead and loaded the cobalt-60 the next day.

The next major task fell to Sylvia Fedoruk—thanks to Allan Blair, the late director of cancer services for the province. Fedoruk's job, and the subject of her master's thesis, was to prepare the rigorous depth-dose measurements for cobalt-60 using lifelike phantoms.[6] It was demanding work that took almost three months to complete, while construction continued around her. Even then, when the Saskatoon unit was officially commissioned on 23 October, the meticulous measurements continued for another two weeks.

This care and precision did not characterize the Western Ontario team, even though it rightly claimed to have been first in the world to treat a patient with cobalt-60. Dr. Ivan H. Smith treated his first patient in London on 27 October, a mere four days after the installation of a machine built by Eldorado Mining and Refining (the prototype of the Atomic Energy of Canada Limited (AECL) cobalt unit).[7] The Ontario patient received a palliative dose, with no hope of a cure, to an approximate area and depth before the unit had been calibrated. The patient did not live long.[8]

Saskatoon, on the other hand, treated its first patient on 8 November 1951. The forty-three-year-old woman, with an advanced cancer unlikely to be cured by any treatment then known, received a precise dose to an exact area. She died, free of cancer, on 26 October 1998 at the age of ninety![9]

The first publication giving details of cobalt-60 therapy appeared incredibly promptly in the prestigious journal, *Nature,* in December 1951. The authors were H. E. Johns, L. M. Bates, E. R. Epp, D. V. Cormack, and S. O. Fedoruk, all physicists from Saskatchewan.[10] The other three authors were Saskatchewan physics graduates, A. Morrison, W. R. Dixon, and C. Garrett, working at the radiology laboratory in the physics division of the National Research Council in Ottawa. The second article, by the same eight physicists, appeared in the equally prestigious journal, *Science,* in March 1952.

More detailed papers on the calibration and use of cobalt-60 filled an entire issue of the *Journal of the Canadian Association of Radiologists* in March 1952 and the depth-dose data appeared in a regular issue and a special supplement to the *British Journal of Radiology* in 1951 and 1952, respectively.[11] The depth-dose charts from Saskatoon were used widely around the world, allowing precise irradiation of a tumour area.[12]

Sylvia Fedoruk has since enjoyed an illustrious career. She served as chief medical physicist for the Saskatoon Cancer Clinic and director of physics services for the Saskatchewan Cancer Foundation, and professor of oncology, University of Saskatchewan.[13] She was also the first woman member of the Atomic Energy Control Board of Canada.[14]

In 1986, Fedoruk was named the first female chancellor of the University of Saskatchewan (1986–89). Two years later, she became the first woman lieutenant-governor of Saskatchewan (1988–94).[15] She is also the recipient of five honorary doctorates,[16] the Queen's Jubilee Medal (1977), and the Taras Shevchenko Medal of the Ukrainian Canadian Congress (1995).[17] She was made an Officer of the Order of

Canada and awarded the Saskatchewan Order of Merit, both in the same year (1986).

But millions of cancer patients worldwide would probably want to thank her for her 1951 master's thesis in physics, simply titled, "Depth-dose." And it all stemmed from the carte blanche approval that Douglas had given Allan Blair and Harold Johns in 1946 to fast track the high energy radiation treatment of cancer.

George Ferguson

He provided the example, but just as important, the inspiration. In 1929, at Dr. R. G. Ferguson's urging, the Saskatchewan government introduced province-wide treatment and diagnosis of tuberculosis, free of charge. It was the first program of its kind in Canada—one of many firsts under Ferguson's direction—and the results were immediate, if not dramatic. Whereas tuberculosis had reached near-epidemic proportions in Saskatchewan in the early twentieth century, Ferguson "galvanized, educated and cajoled an entire province ... [to a degree] unequalled anywhere else on the continent."[1] The Imperial Order Daughters of the Empire raised money for special needs, rural Homemakers' Clubs donated chickens and eggs, local radio stations held weekly amateur hours, and Christmas Seals were sold by Traveller's guilds.[2]

The lesson was not lost on Tommy Douglas, who came to power as CCF premier in 1944 determined to provide better health care for the province's citizens. Here was a universal plan that had not only dramatically reduced the prevalence of a once-common disease, but had been successfully financed for the past fifteen years by municipal and provincial taxes. It gave Douglas the courage and the confidence to go forward with his own plans for universal hospitalization and then medicare.

Robert George Ferguson, the sixth of fourteen children, was born near
South Joliette, North Dakota, on 12 September 1883. At nineteen,
he was delegated by his family to find a farm across the border in
Saskatchewan and selected one just south of Yorkton. Four years later,
following the death of his father in 1906, George was dividing his
time between running the farm in summer and securing a university
education during the winter months. He obtained his B.A. from Wesley College in Winnipeg in 1910, intending to enter the ministry, but
his post-diphtheria voice could not handle the strain of preaching.
He turned to medicine instead and graduated from the University of
Manitoba in 1916.[3]

Ferguson's medical training included a minimum two-week internship in a tuberculosis sanatorium. The M.D. degree was withheld
at Manitoba until student doctors had gained some practical experience in dealing with the greatest health problem of the day.[4] Tuberculosis, or consumption as it was earlier known, killed or disabled
more Canadians than any other affliction, including heart disease and
cancer. Many of its victims were in the prime of their lives.

Ferguson completed his tuberculosis training with Dr. David A.
Stewart, medical superintendent at the Ninette Sanatorium. The experience had a decisive influence on his future career. Not only did
Ferguson find his lifelong calling, but when Saskatchewan opened its
first tuberculosis sanatorium at Fort Qu'Appelle in 1917, Stewart recommended him for the superintendent position. He recognized that
Ferguson, slightly older and more mature than most of his classmates,
had both clinical skills and administrative smarts.[5] Both would be
needed to meet the challenge ahead.

Tuberculosis was quite common in early twentieth-century Saskatchewan. The overcrowding of large farm families in small homestead
shacks, especially during the long, cold prairie winters, proved ideal
breeding grounds for the disease. Few suspected what was wrong,
apart from a persistent cough. Before the widespread advent of x-ray
machines, symptoms were insidious and non-specific; many victims
were in the advanced stage before a correct diagnosis was made.

Ferguson (named Muskeke-O-Kemacan or Great White Physician) was determined to eradicate and prevent the spread of tuberculosis in Saskatchewan's First Nations population.
SASKATCHEWAN LUNG ASSOCIATION

The disease also stalked the province's First Nations population. Here, the incidence was made worse by poverty and malnutrition— and the fact that it went largely unchecked. Saskatchewan reserves had the dubious distinction of having some of the highest mortality rates from tuberculosis. Ferguson's statistical study of this "virgin-soil" epidemic remains "one of the best of a very few epidemiologic accounts of such a process anywhere in the world."[6]

It was the First World War, though, that finally brought home the seriousness of the problem. Indeed, the war, with all its vicissitudes, proved to be less the enemy than a saviour in disguise. Many returning veterans had acquired active or infectious tuberculosis in the trenches of France. And before they could be safely reintegrated into Canadian society, they required immediate treatment. The federal government consequently provided the funding to build more sanatoria and care for more patients.

Saskatchewan was a clear beneficiary of this federal initiative. The Fort Qu'Appelle Sanatorium (popularly known as Fort San) was in 1917 the first of three provincial treatment facilities to open. At the time, there was no specific treatment available for tuberculosis, only rest, fresh air, and good food. Sanatoria provided these, but the process was slow and expensive. One major benefit of sanatoria was that those patients with "open," highly infective tuberculosis, coughing up sputum that was teeming with bacilli, were isolated from their families and the general public, which reduced the spread of disease.

As the only doctor initially hired at Fort San, Ferguson was on call twenty-four hours a day. He was known to sit up all night holding the hand of a dying patient.[7] But there was only so much his strength of purpose and compassion could do, and he took it upon himself to make the province a leader in the fight against the disease. He started with educating politicians and gave a personal tour of the sanatorium to thirty members of the provincial legislature in November 1920. Less than a year later, the Martin government established the Saskatchewan Anti-tuberculosis Commission to determine the prevalence of the disease among the provincial population and decide on a course of action. It was no coincidence that Ferguson was named commission secretary.[8]

Over the next decade, Ferguson pioneered a number of firsts. As part of the research for the provincial commission, a sample of over one thousand school children in seven representative Saskatchewan communities was examined for tuberculosis. No other jurisdiction in Canada had conducted similar baseline studies. Nor did Ferguson stop there. In September 1923, the province sponsored the country's first travelling TB clinics.[9]

Ferguson was also intent on eradicating and preventing the disease in the province's First Nations population. He secured research funding to examine children at nearby Indian residential schools. He also joined the 1927 treaty party and conducted chest radiographs on all adult Indians. And he engineered an agreement with the federal government in 1924 to provide sanatorium beds for First Nations patients—another first in Canada.[10]

Ferguson would spearhead other groundbreaking initiatives, including the BCG vaccination of Native infants and student nurses, a province-wide radiographic survey for tuberculosis, and sufficient hospital beds to treat all tuberculosis patients. But his greatest accomplishment—one that he had spent the better part of a decade tirelessly working for—was the passage of provincial legislation providing for the free treatment of tuberculosis, effective 1 January 1929.[11] The significance of this achievement was underscored by the fact that the disease was not only the most expensive to treat, but took the longest to cure. Ferguson was also lucky. Less than a year later, Saskatchewan was brought to its knees by the double whammy of drought and depression. It is doubtful that the legislation would have been approved under such circumstances.

Dr. R. G. Ferguson's battle against the scourge of tuberculosis paid immediate dividends. Premier Tommy Douglas thought so highly of the anti-tuberculosis crusader that he recommended that Ferguson be named lieutenant-governor upon his retirement in 1948. Ottawa ignored the suggestion.

But Ferguson contributed to Saskatchewan in a much more important way during Douglas's tenure as premier. His championing of free, province-wide treatment of tuberculosis was a necessary first step in the eventual introduction of medicare. He also made the impossible seem possible. In 1961, at the fiftieth anniversary of the founding of the Saskatchewan Anti-tuberculosis League, Douglas observed that the people of the province had "a special capacity to meet and solve problems that by far excels more fortunate places."[12] He clearly had Ferguson in mind that day.

Ertle Harrington

By all accounts, Ertle Harrington was quite the character—the epitome of the absent-minded professor, an American whom one student described as "more English than the English." Even his first name seemed right out of a Dr. Seuss children's book. But it was his inventive nature that enabled him to give Saskatchewan an early leadership role in the fight against cancer.

Recruited by the University of Saskatchewan in 1920, Harrington quickly turned the Department of Physics into a leader in radiation physics for the next half-century. He also reached outside the academy to collaborate with cancer physicians in Saskatchewan in the fight against the deadly disease. According to a former graduate student, "he can probably be considered Canada's first medical physicist." [1]

Ertle Leslie Harrington was born in Bucklin, Missouri, in 1887 and educated in that state. He received an M.A. from Harvard in 1915 and a Ph.D. from the University of Chicago a year later. Harrington then did post-doctoral work in radiation physics under the direction of R. A. Millikan, one of the world's foremost physicists. Harrington's project was to make a precise measurement of the viscosity of air, a key ingredient in Millikan's "oil-drop" method for determining the electric charge on an electron.

Professor Ertle Harrington produced radioactive "gold seeds" in the University of Saskatchewan Physics Department for use in the Regina and Saskatoon Cancer Clinics.

UNIVERSITY OF SASKATCHEWAN ARCHIVES A3191

Harrington joined the Department of Physics at the University of Saskatchewan in 1920 and became head of the department four years later, a position he held until his retirement in 1952.[2] The hiring of the eccentric physicist was a real coup for the university—something that President Walter Murray was apparently anxious to exploit, especially after he learned that radium was being used for cancer treatment in Quebec. The president wrote Saskatchewan Liberal Premier Charles Dunning in October 1922, offering the services of the university's physicists if the government decided to offer cancer treatment to the province's citizens. Dunning replied that the eradication of tuberculosis was a greater health priority in Saskatchewan. He also added that "the possibility of successful use of radium in any large way in the treatment of disease has not been fully demonstrated."[3]

By the end of the decade, though, a new government headed by Conservative leader J. T. M. Anderson was in power in Regina, and it was committed, in the words of the Health minister, to having Saskatchewan "lead the way in Canada ... in dealing with the cancer problem."[4] To this end, the Saskatchewan Medical Association established a cancer commission in 1929 to provide advice to the government on how best to proceed. Harrington was invited to join the committee as the only non-medical member. His involvement marked "the natural association between radium supply and cancer control" that was the hallmark of the Saskatchewan experience.[5]

The SMA's cancer committee was determined to advance the cause of radiotherapy in the province. At that time, only a few Saskatchewan doctors had purchased tiny amounts of radium, and the doses they were able to deliver to cancer patients were little more than homeopathic. It made more sense, from Harrington's perspective, if the provincial government secured a larger amount of radium, at least half a gram, for use in two treatment centres: one in Regina, the other Saskatoon. This recommendation was incorporated into the March 1930 Saskatchewan Cancer Commission Act that established the Saskatchewan Cancer Commission. It was the first cancer control agency of its kind in Canada and probably the first in North America.[6]

One of the first tasks of the new Saskatchewan Cancer Commission was to decide where the government-purchased radium was to be stored and how it was to be made available to the two provincial cancer clinics. Once again, Harrington provided the solution. He not only convinced the cancer commission that the University of Saskatchewan was a secure location to store the radium bromide, but that the plant for extracting radon (radium emanation) for cancer treatment should be built in the Physics Department. Harrington apparently likened the radon plant to a dairy to justify the university location for the production and distribution of the radon.[7]

But who was going to build the plant and collect the radon gas? That, too, fell to Harrington. After checking into the cost of apparatus available on the market and inspecting several radon plants in the United States during his 1930 Christmas holidays, the physicist concluded that it would be more economical, especially when the province was mired in the Great Depression, if he designed and constructed his own radon plant. It was said that Harrington was "a confirmed gadgeteer who could never pass by a rubbish pile without rescuing an item of potential use in the lab."[8]

Harrington started work on the project once classes were over in the spring of 1931. He was ready that fall to load the radium bromide that had arrived in Saskatoon by special rail car in six glass tubes in a lead case. This transfer was the most dangerous part of the operation, but after rehearsing the procedure several times, the radium solution was safely installed in the plant. "We sure were happy that all went well for us," recounted a somewhat relieved instrument-maker in the Physics Department.[9]

With the plant operational, the next step was to extract the radon gas that emanated from the radium bromide solution. Here, Harrington's remarkable skills as a glass blower came to the fore. The radioactive gas was pumped into fine glass tubing, prepared by Harrington, which in turn was connected to fine gold tubing by sealing wax. A technician, usually a student, would compress the radon into the gold tubing and then cut it into lengths, or "seeds" as they were known.

Harrington supplied the radioactive gold seeds, which had a 3.8-day half-life, to the Regina and Saskatoon Cancer Clinics, as well as to treatment facilities in other provinces.[10] It had been found that faster-growing cancer cells could be destroyed by radiation. The seeds were consequently implanted, often permanently, directly into cancerous tissue, especially tumours of the cervix, uterus, and tongue.[11] Hundreds of people benefited from this treatment, albeit in many cases for only a few years.

Ertle Harrington retired from the university in 1952 and died four years later in Oakland, California. Ironically, his homemade radon plant outlived him by six years. By 1962, after more than thirty years of operation, compounded by repeated doses of radiation, the plant had to be shut down because of a small leak.

Harrington and his radioactive seeds might seem light-years away from the treatment of cancer today. But the bringing together of physicists and physicians, as personified by Harrington's career, was exactly the kind of collaboration that put Saskatchewan at the forefront of radiotherapy and medical physics.[12] It was also representative of the spirit and innovation that Premier Tommy Douglas sought to draw upon when the new CCF government passed the Cancer Control Act during its very first legislative session. As of November 1944, the province provided free diagnosis and treatment of cancer. This step on the road to medicare would not have been possible without visionaries like Harrington.[13]

Orville Hjertaas

He was a pariah to many in his association. In October 1961, Dr. Orville Hjertaas of Prince Albert was one of the few practising physicians who *publicly* supported the Tommy Douglas government when it introduced the Saskatchewan Medical Care Insurance bill. Hjertaas not only agreed to serve on the provincial commission charged with implementing the legislation, but also refused to join the bitter doctors' strike that rocked the province. In defiance of the College of Physicians and Surgeons, he continued to offer his services to the public through one of the province's first community clinics.

Hjertaas's brazen actions were not some spur of the moment decision, made in the heat of the moment when forced to declare himself. Some fifteen years earlier, as a health region organizer, he had helped take the first tentative steps toward the introduction of medicare.

Orville Kenneth Hjertaas was born 31 May 1917 in Wauchope in southeastern Saskatchewan near the interprovincial border with Manitoba. His Norwegian parents, Martin and Alma, had settled in the area two years earlier, and the homestead is still in the family today. They were founding members of the Saskatchewan Wheat Pool and were also involved in the co-operative movement. Come the Great

Dr. Orville Hjertaas of Prince Albert was one of the few practising physicians who publicly supported the Tommy Douglas government when it introduced the Saskatchewan Medical Care Insurance bill. SASKATCHEWAN ARCHIVES BOARD S-B7382

Depression, the Hjertaas family embraced the new Co-operative Commonwealth Federation Party and its call for reform.

Orville took his first two years of medicine at the University of Saskatchewan and then his clinical studies at the University of Manitoba. Upon graduation in 1942, he did a year of pathology at the Winnipeg General Hospital, followed by a year of rest at the Fort Qu'Appelle Sanatorium to treat the tuberculosis he had contracted. He then practised general medicine in Wauchope before joining the new Health Services Planning Commission on 1 September 1945 as regional organizer for health regions.

Hjertaas's appointment was a direct outcome of the October 1944 Sigerist report, which had recommended that health care services be decentralized in the province because of the predominantly rural population. The new CCF government had immediately established the Planning Commission to oversee, among other things, the creation of fourteen health districts in the province; each regional health board, in turn, would be responsible for managing and providing local care. As district organizer, Hjertaas spent much of his time on the road—meeting with community leaders, helping to decide on regional boundaries, and getting regional boards created.

This experience left a lasting impression on Hjertaas. He had to hit the ground running in his new position to keep up with what was happening in the Swift Current region. On 15 September 1945, only two weeks into his job, Hjertaas attended the organizational meeting where Bill Burak of the Rural Municipality of Pittville had convinced rural and municipal representatives from the southwest to come together to talk about the formation of a health region that would offer a comprehensive package of health services. Fully aware that Premier Douglas and the Planning Commission did not want the new district to take on too much at the beginning, Hjertaas tried to convince the delegates to give priority first to preventive services and pushed for more doctors, hospital beds, and diagnostic equipment.[1] But over the course of the meeting, he came to appreciate that the scheme was first and foremost a local initiative, and that the region, and not Regina, had to decide what services would be offered.

This need for prospective health regions to have a say in, if not determine, their own health services mandate was driven home in the next two months as Orville Hjertaas, along with Tommy McLeod and Mrs. A. M. Lydiard of the Planning Commission, travelled the back roads of southern Saskatchewan in preparation for a late November vote on the formation of health regions in the Swift Current (#1) and Weyburn-Estevan (#3) districts.[2] It would become readily apparent to Hjertaas why municipal officials like Burak were pushing for something more than preventive care.

During October and November 1945, Hjertaas held thirty-eight meetings—on average at least one every other day—in the Swift Current and Weyburn-Estevan districts.[3] Although his role as an organizer was to encourage a strong and positive vote in favour of the new health regions, he also collected information about the general health of the population for the Health Service Planning Commission. It was a distressing exercise—even for someone who had been born and raised in rural Saskatchewan.

In his official report to Dr. Mindel C. Sheps, then chair of the Planning Commission, Hjertaas began by expressing his "dismay at the deplorable health services that exist … hospital facilities … hopelessly inadequately equipped."[4] "Wherever I travel," he continued, "I find cases of crippling disease and disability that could be cured … of permanent disability from preventable or curable conditions."[5]

There was no shortage of examples of how bad things were. "The people of Consul and Govenlock," he noted, "are over 60 miles from the nearest doctor."[6] At Prelate, he interviewed a man whose fourteen-year-old son had "abscesses of the lung requiring resection of the left lower lobe"; the local doctor had told him that it would be "useless for him to see the specialist until he has $1,500 in cash."[7]

His most damning comments were directed at a system where a family's ability to pay, and not the patient's condition, mattered more. "Finally a very serious drawback to good medical service is the present system of fee for service," he observed. "Under this system the very rich and the very poor for whom the municipality pays, get all the laboratory, x-ray work and consultant service that they require. The great mass of the people cannot afford this very expensive investigation and the Doctor who must decide whether to order it or not, is debating in his own mind, the possibility of his even being able to collect his own fee if he puts the patient to the expense of this investigation."[8]

In general, Hjertaas found the people "grasping for anything that holds any promise of improvement in their Health Services."[9] He asked rhetorically: "Are the people of the province of Saskatchewan justified in persisting in the inhuman cruelty of making our citizens walk through life in the constant sight of their invalid[ed] offspring, tortured by the knowledge that they are unable to provide the necessary silver to make them well?"[10]

The answer was forthcoming on 26 November 1945. Weyburn-Estevan voted overwhelmingly (6,264 for; 2,419 against) for a regional plan for preventive health services only.[11] Swift Current, on the other hand, endorsed a more ambitious regional scheme for complete medical services.[12]

Hjertaas attended the first meeting of the new board of Swift Current Health Region #1, held at Gull Lake early in the new year.[13] He briefly described the Sigerist plan for the promotion of regional health services and then suggested that the district be divided into four quadrants, based respectively on the largest town or city in each: Leader, Maple Creek, Swift Current, and Shaunavon.[14] This proposal was accepted, as well as a more important motion confirming that Swift Current would be a full-service health region. Hjertaas realized that he was witnessing health service history. "[It is] very hard to adequately express the spirit of cooperation and unity of purpose that prevailed," he recalled, "a most gratifying experience to be able to attend this meeting and to see these men at work."[15]

Orville Hjertaas became secretary of the Health Service Planning Commission in early February 1946. He held the position until August when he joined two fellow University of Manitoba medical classmates who had just returned from the war and started a general practice in Prince Albert. They enjoyed a successful practice together for fifteen years until they found themselves on opposing sides during the 1961–62 medicare crisis.

Premier Douglas would often visit Orville when he was in Prince Albert. Hjertaas's wife Millie was expected to provide meals. Supper was not a problem, but one time she asked Tommy what he would like for breakfast. "Oatmeal porridge, of course," replied Douglas. But Millie had never made oatmeal porridge. A lawyer's wife and friend, Mary MacIsaac,[16] provided Millie with a crash course in porridge-making; Tommy, after next morning's breakfast, praised Millie, none the wiser.

In January 1989, Hjertaas was named Prince Albert's Citizen of the Year. He received the Saskatchewan Order of Merit, the province's highest honour, in 1993 and became a Member of the Order of Canada four years later. He died in Prince Albert on 23 May 1998.[17] His memory lives on in the Prince Albert community clinic, which, in keeping with his earlier work as a health region organizer, "pioneered group practice arrangements as well as an approach to health care delivery which emphasized prevention."[18]

Kiyoshi Izumi

⚛

He became known as the architect who took hallucinogenic drugs in order to bring greater sensitivity to his work. In May 1965, in response to growing questions about the medical use of LSD, the *New York Times* carried an article about Kiyoshi Izumi and how he had regularly used the drug on an experimental basis in Weyburn, Saskatchewan, to develop a new design for mental hospitals.

Readers of the article might have scoffed at the idea, especially at a time when the recreational use of the drug, more popularly known as acid, was increasingly seen as a menace. But the newspaper looked favourably on what Izumi had been trying to achieve a decade earlier in Saskatchewan—a design that "merged therapeutic principles with humane care in a manner that avoided the 'insensitive, hygienic, well-regulated hopelessness' that … characterized contemporary mental hospitals."[1] That Izumi was able to develop such a model owed much to the Tommy Douglas government and the exciting research atmosphere that pervaded the Weyburn hospital in the 1950s. At the time, Izumi was "probably the only architect in the world who [could] communicate better with psychiatrists than with architects."[2]

Kiyoshi Izumi, known to his friends as Joe, was born in Vancouver on 24 March 1921. Fortunately, he was away from British Columbia dur-

Izumi (with Francis Huxley) worked on plans for a new mental hospital design, Weyburn 1958.
SASKATCHEWAN ARCHIVES BOARD R-PS-58-056-04

ing the Second World War; otherwise, he would have joined the thousands of persons of Japanese ancestry, including the Canadian-born, who were forcibly evacuated from the Pacific coast in February 1942.

Kiyoshi studied at Regina College and then entered the School of Architecture at the University of Manitoba. He was a scholarship student—capped off with the university gold medal upon graduation in 1948. There followed graduate work at a number of prestigious schools: the London School of Economics, the Massachusetts Institute of Technology, and Harvard University. He returned to Regina in 1953, where he entered into private architectural practice with fellow student Gordon Arnott.[3] In post-war Saskatchewan, he found an activist CCF government with an ambitious legislative agenda, including a bill of rights against racial and religious discrimination. Equally important, he found a place where his interest in environmental design was to find full expression.

In 1954, Izumi was asked by the provincial government to serve as an advisor on re-conceptualizing and re-designing the province's mental hospitals. Premier Douglas wanted to ensure that mental health issues were given the same kind of attention as the physical well-being of the Saskatchewan population. The provincial director of psychiatric services, Dr. Griff McKerracher, was also pushing for significant changes in how the province handled mental illness. It was expected that Izumi would not only critically assess the current facilities, from a design and layout perspective, but also suggest how the hospital environment could be modified to accommodate patient needs.

This investigation meant that Izumi worked closely with Dr. Humphry Osmond, superintendent of the Weyburn mental hospital. Osmond headed an experimental program that used LSD to simulate schizophrenia; by understanding how individuals with the disorder experienced or perceived their environment, Osmond reasoned, researchers would be better able to understand the disease. The psychiatrist also maintained that the hospital setting affected schizophrenics since these individuals "perceived reality in a fundamentally different way from 'normal' individuals" and that any design must take into consideration patient sensibilities.[4]

Izumi was won over by Osmond's arguments. It was one thing to declare that the Weyburn facility was overcrowded, inadequate, and outdated, but exactly how did schizophrenics view their hospital environment? And how could that environment be made less threatening, more therapeutic? To find out, Izumi took LSD, as did his wife, Amy. "I perceived that the world was turning," Izumi described his first experience with the drug, "and my immediate reaction was I was in one of Van Gogh's paintings."[5]

Thereafter, Izumi regularly used LSD to try to understand how individuals suffering from schizophrenia reacted to the colours, shapes, and other features of their hospital setting. These experiences were then used to come up with a design that was comforting for patients and thereby more conducive for treatment and healing. Izumi likened it to "psychic space," a term that may not have been as catchy as "psychedelic," but one that nicely captured the architectural approach he was trying to promote.[6]

This concept of psychic space was given a further boost when Dr. Robert Sommer, a behavioural psychologist from Kansas, arrived in Weyburn in 1957. Sommer immediately commenced a study of the hospital, its patients, and staff, and found that incarceration in the large, imposing mental hospital produced counter-productive habits in patients that were difficult to break even after they were discharged. Long-term hospitalization, Sommer insisted, spawned a new disease, which he called "disculturation" or institutionalization. The solution was to provide patients with a small-group living environment as near as possible to home conditions, including privacy and a place for personal possessions.[7]

This collaboration between Izumi, Osmond, and Sommer culminated in a submission to the World Health Organization for funding to develop a new mental hospital design. Over one hundred proposals were considered in the 1958 international competition. But in the end, the Saskatchewan entry—a circular structure designed by Izumi—was one of only four to be selected. The round building, with private patient rooms around the perimeter, was applauded for its innovative combination of therapeutic needs and spatial features—a blurring of medical and non-medical functions. It seemed to herald a new era in institutional care, ironically inspired, in part, by LSD.

Bringing the plan to reality, though, was another matter. Although the Izumi design was supposed to be used for a series of regional mental health facilities, it was used only once in Saskatchewan, and even then, it was modified.

In 1960, the Douglas government approved the construction of the Izumi-inspired Yorkton Psychiatric Centre. The timing of the announcement proved problematic, since the new 190-bed Yorkton Union Hospital was already under construction. It consequently cost an additional seven hundred thousand dollars to change the design of both buildings, which were to be connected by a passageway with glass walls. In the process, the Izumi circular design was replaced by the more traditional rectangular shape. Further delays meant that it was not until March 1962 that work on the Psychiatric Centre actually began.[8]

The completed facility consisted of five one-storey, connected cottages with a total of 132 one-patient rooms, each with a window looking out on vacant space. Colour was skilfully used throughout the building to create a "general feeling of freedom, repose and well-being."[9] It was somewhat ironic that Tommy Douglas, whose CCF government's per capita expenditures for mental health in his final year as premier far exceeded that of any other province,[10] set the stage for a new Liberal Minister of Health, Davey Steuart, to give the dedication address at the official Yorkton opening in June 1964. It was quite fitting, though, that Dr. Humphry Osmond, now working in New Jersey, gave the banquet address, while Izumi proudly looked on.

Kiyoshi Izumi left private practice in 1968 to become a faculty member with the Environmental Studies Department at the Regina campus of the University of Saskatchewan. That was the same year he was awarded a prestigious Killam Fellowship. Other honours followed, including election as a Fellow of the Royal Architectural Institute of Canada and appointment to the Royal Canadian Academy of the Arts, before his death in 1996.

Like other architects, Izumi's legacy lives on in the many buildings he designed, such as the Regina Public Library or Marquis Hall on the University of Saskatchewan campus. He was also at the forefront of his discipline, though, in challenging the post-war trend toward buildings that essentially alienated individuals from society—something that found expression during his days in Weyburn. This work may not have meant the end of mental hospitals. But the new LSD-inspired design nonetheless "went well beyond matters of brick and mortar and … went to great lengths to try and appreciate how patients understood their environment and … worked across disciplines."[11]

Harold Johns

It was a bold, perhaps even impetuous, decision, based largely on faith—faith in the two scientists proposing the idea, faith in the new technology, and faith in Saskatchewan becoming the world leader in cancer treatment.

In early fall 1946, Dr. Allan Blair, director of Saskatchewan Cancer Services for the province, and Dr. Harold Johns, a young physics professor, called on Premier Tommy Douglas at his Regina office. The pair came unannounced, and were given a 10 A.M. appointment. Tommy listened in rapt attention as they explained how they wanted to purchase a betatron, a new high-energy radiation source, to treat cancer patients in the province. The premier, who also held the Health portfolio in the CCF government, gave Blair and Johns virtual carte blanche to proceed—without consulting his cabinet, the university, or even medical experts.

It might be tempting to dismiss this story as nothing more than apocryphal folklore, part of the Douglas legend. But during a brief interview in the back seat of a car in February 1983, the former Saskatchewan premier not only confirmed that he made the momentous decision on the spur of the moment, but explained why. "Well, it was easy," he clearly recounted. "I had complete confidence in the knowledge and the integrity possessed by both men. They assured me that

Harold Johns pioneered the use of cobalt-60 for cancer treatment for Saskatchewan.
SASKATCHEWAN CANCER COMMISSION

high voltage radiotherapy offered great promise in the treatment of cancer. Dr. Allan Blair had come from Toronto to head up the leading cancer agency in North America. And Harold Johns! Why, when I attended Brandon College, Alfred Edward Johns [his father] was my mathematics teacher and my favourite professor … So, with my close personal knowledge of both men and my complete faith in their integrity, my permission did not seem to me to be a gamble at all." [1]

Harold Elford Johns was born 4 July 1915 in a Buddhist temple in Chengdu, China, to missionary parents Alfred and Myrtle (Madge) Johns. Alfred taught mathematics and his wife taught English at West China University in Szechuan (now Sichuan) province for sixteen years before civil strife forced them to return to North America in 1925, first to Tacoma, Washington, and then Brandon, Manitoba. [2] Tommy Douglas got to know the Johns family during his student days at Brandon College in the latter half of the 1920s and remembered that young Harold "showed great promise." [3] Harold also had a strong sense of purpose, most likely nurtured by his Asian childhood in a strict Methodist household.

Johns attended McMaster University, where he obtained a B.Sc. in mathematics and physics in 1936, followed by an M.A. and Ph.D. in physics at the University of Toronto in 1937 and 1939, respectively. [4] Johns had been awarded an 1851 Research Scholarship at Cambridge University in England, often considered the scientific equivalent of a Rhodes, but he was unable to accept it because the Second World War began. He consequently spent the war as an instructor at the University of Alberta Radar School. Here, he taught physics, mathematics, and navigation to pilots in the British Commonwealth Air Training Plan. To test for metal fatigue, he placed an aircraft propeller on a large x-ray film for several hours beneath a radium needle that spread high-energy radiation in all directions. [5]

This practical experience as a radiation physicist soon found another application next door in Saskatchewan. In October 1944, the new CCF government established a North American first by providing for the free diagnosis and treatment of cancer under the Cancer Control Act. Dr. Allan Blair, the new director of cancer services for Saskatchewan, looked upon the legislation as an unprecedented opportunity to wage battle against the disease, one that was best fought with a full-time radiation physicist. In his very first official letter, then, he proposed to Professor Ertle Harrington, head of physics at the

University of Saskatchewan, that the university and the Saskatchewan Cancer Commission co-operate and jointly appoint a faculty member to teach physics and supervise, half-time, the radium and x-ray therapy equipment at the two Saskatchewan cancer clinics. Harrington readily embraced the idea and secured Johns's appointment, effective March 1945. Johns effectively became Canada's first full-time cancer physicist.[6]

Harold Johns took it upon himself to develop the most effective form of cancer treatment for the province. To this end, he secured an eight-hundred-dollar travel scholarship to visit the leading radiation centres in Canada and the United States and talk to cancer scientists during the summer of 1946. While in Toronto, he attended a series of lectures by Professor M. V. Mayneord of the Royal Cancer Hospital in London, England. Mayneord was one of the first to suggest the possibility of using cobalt-60 as a practical radiation source.[7]

Johns returned to Saskatchewan full of enthusiasm about the potential of cobalt-60. So, too, was Ertle Harrington, who predicted that the new radioactive isotope "may become a more suitable source than radium itself in the treatment of cancer."[8] But for the time being, Johns decided that the betatron, already under development in the United States, offered more immediate promise.

At Allan Blair's prodding, Johns asked that a betatron be secured for the University of Saskatchewan Physics Department for use by the Saskatoon cancer clinic. It came with a hefty price tag—eighty thousand dollars. That's why Blair and Johns decided to see Premier Douglas and get his support for the initiative. A subsequent application for funding to the Atomic Energy Board secured less than half the required amount. Johns was disappointed, but Blair was ecstatic. "Spend that money, Johns," he instructed. "When it is gone more will be found."[9]

In late April 1948, Johns travelled to the Allis-Chalmers plant in Milwaukee, Wisconsin, to inspect the 24-MeV betatron that had been built for Saskatchewan. It would be almost another year, following installation and nine months of precise calibration and evaluation, before the first patient was treated. But when that finally happened on 29 March 1949, it marked "the first concerted clinical use of the betatron in the world."[10] The University of Saskatchewan betatron provided a method of delivering a high radiation dose to tumours deep in the human body, without appreciably damaging the overlying skin, and with a lower risk of radiation sickness, blood damage, and other side effects.[11]

The betatron had a downside, though. It proved expensive to operate (only 301 patients were treated in a seventeen-year period), while its campus location was incredibly inconvenient for patients and medical staff who had to travel from City Hospital on the other side of the river. After only three months of betatron treatments to his credit, Johns decided to pursue cobalt-60 as a more economical way to deliver high-energy cancer treatment.

Johns started this new quest in June 1949 by first visiting the National Research Council NRX reactor at Chalk River, Ontario, the only installation in the world then capable of producing sufficiently intense sources of radioactive cobalt. He then secured the permission of the university president to proceed with the development of his "cobalt bomb" on the understanding that it was essentially a research project. There followed a simple, three-page application to the NRC for the cobalt-60 isotope. Just weeks later, three radioactive cobalt sources were placed in the Chalk River pile to "cook."

Johns installed the cobalt-60 source in the still incomplete new wing of the University Hospital in Saskatoon on 17 August 1951. Once the unit was officially commissioned on 23 October, the existing 400-kilovolt radiotherapy machine was immediately obsolete. And no wonder! Johns's cobalt bomb "was one-tenth as large, delivered radiation at 10 times the energy and at 10 times the rate" as what was then being used to treat cancer.[12]

In 1956, Harold Johns was lured to Toronto to be head of the physics division of the Ontario Cancer Institute and, two years later, head of the Department of Medical Biophysics at the University of Toronto. He wrote four editions (1953–83) of the world's foremost textbook in medical radiation physics, *The Physics of Radiology*, which was also translated into Spanish, Russian, and Chinese.[13] Johns received many honours,[14] but he was especially proud of being made an Officer of the Order of Canada in 1978. He retired in 1980 and died in Kingston, Ontario, on 23 August 1998.

Johns was inducted posthumously into the Canadian Medical Hall of Fame, the first medical physicist to be so honoured, on 28 October 1998. It was entirely fitting that the late Tommy Douglas was inducted that same evening, represented by his daughter Shirley and her son, the Hollywood movie actor Kiefer Sutherland.[15] As Johns himself reminisced about his fateful meeting with Douglas, "I wonder if anyone could be so lucky today—to find a politician so eager to help."[16]

Al Johnson

He was a leading member of the "Saskatchewan Mafia." No, not farmers in pinstripe coveralls with Italian accents and five o'clock shadows, but civil servants who lost their jobs or resigned their positions when Liberal leader Ross Thatcher chased the New Democratic Party from office in the 1964 provincial election. Al Johnson, a former deputy treasurer (1952–64) in the Tommy Douglas and later Woodrow Lloyd governments, was among them.

These former Saskatchewan bureaucrats, who had brought about a revolution in how government functioned, infiltrated governments across the country—hence their nickname. In New Brunswick, for example, they helped Liberal Premier Louis Robichaud initiate what is sometimes known as the "other quiet revolution." Their more pervasive influence, though, was in Ottawa, where they were largely responsible for the introduction of the modern welfare state during Lester Pearson's tenure as prime minister.

Al Johnson had a direct hand in several new federal programs—from equalization to post-secondary education funding to medicare—in his capacity as the new assistant deputy minister of Finance. He was able to assume such a critical role because of the experience he brought from his days as a senior manager in the Saskatchewan public service. It was also a direct consequence of his family's strong sense of public duty.

Albert Wesley Johnson was born at Insinger, Saskatchewan, on 18 October 1923. His father, a Methodist minister and Great War veteran, was at the time involved in the Insinger experiment, a Christian home mission that sought to Canadianize the district's large Ukrainian population.

It was through the church that Johnson first came to know Tommy Douglas, the young, diminutive Baptist preacher from Weyburn. Once a year in the early 1930s, after the family had moved to Wilcox, Johnson would be treated to a Douglas sermon in his father's United Church. Douglas (who, not at all hidebound by minor differences of doctrine and practice between denominations, had earned his way through divinity at Baptist Brandon College by preaching in a Presbyterian Church) saw that Al was unusually bright for his age, with great promise.

So, too, did J. S. Woodsworth, leader of the federal Co-operative Commonwealth Federation Party and one of Douglas's mentors. In 1941, an ailing Woodsworth invited the seventeen-year-old Johnson, then a University of Saskatchewan student working in British Columbia for the summer, to visit him at his Vancouver home. He knew the elder Johnson from his days in theology school in Winnipeg before the war and wanted to talk to the young man about his future. After reminiscing about his career as a Christian social democrat, Woodsworth directly asked Johnson to consider a political career if he wanted to bring about a better world.

Johnson chose neither religion nor politics. After completing his undergraduate degree at Saskatchewan, he did a stint in the Canadian Army in 1942 before pursuing a master's degree in political science at the University of Toronto. He was hired immediately upon graduation by the year-old CCF government in Saskatchewan. It was the beginning of a long and illustrious civil service career.

Al Johnson started working for the Saskatchewan government in the Adult Education Division in 1945. But within a year, Tommy McLeod, economic advisor to the Douglas cabinet, found a better use for Johnson's considerable talents and had him transferred to the newly created Budget Bureau. By 1949, Johnson was the director of

Al Johnson saw government as a modernizing force in society and sought to develop a professional public service in Saskatchewan that valued and encouraged creative ways of doing things.
SASKATCHEWAN ARCHIVES BOARD R-B6094

administrative management of the Budget Bureau, and from 1952 to 1964, deputy provincial treasurer and secretary to the Treasury Board for the government of Saskatchewan.

Johnson worked hand in glove with provincial Treasurer Clarence Fines, who faced the competing demands of fulfilling the new government's ambitious reform program and getting the province's finances in order after the Great Depression and Second World War. It was a delicate balancing act, but he delivered a remarkable string of sixteen consecutive balanced budgets—thanks, in no small part, to people like Johnson who staffed the Provincial Treasurer Department.

Fines was often criticized within the party for putting the brakes on CCF initiatives. But the provincial treasurer and the people who worked for him understood and appreciated the need to ensure that any new developments were financially possible. Indeed, Fines and Johnson had tremendous respect for one another, a situation that enabled both men to concentrate on what they did best.

In Johnson's case, it meant not only overseeing the operations of the Provincial Treasurer Department, but also actively recruiting young university graduates from across the country to become part of the bold Saskatchewan experiment. Johnson saw government as a modernizing force in society and sought to develop a professional public service in Saskatchewan that valued and encouraged creative ways of doing things. It led to what has been called "a 'matrix of trust' within Saskatchewan's nascent civil service."[1]

This idea of "government as a positive catalyst of change"[2] can be seen in Johnson's membership on the interdepartmental committee that was charged with bringing about a universal and comprehensive medical insurance plan in Saskatchewan. It was also readily apparent during his subsequent Ottawa career, most notably as economic advisor to Prime Minister Trudeau on the Constitution (1968–70) and as president of the Canadian Broadcasting Corporation (1975–82).[3] Johnson even promoted his idea of governance in the international arena when he served as a public administration consultant first in Indonesia and then South Africa in the 1990s.

Al Johnson retired in 1999 as one of Canada's greatest civil servants.[4] But in keeping with his sense of public duty, he took on one more major task.

In 1963, while on educational leave at Harvard University, Johnson completed his doctorate on the Douglas government's years in power in Saskatchewan. The dissertation, plainly titled "The Biography of a Government: Policy Formation in Saskatchewan, 1944–1961," sought to serve as "a case study of the art and practice of governing."[5]

Although Johnson was "possibly the most published civil servant in Canada,"[6] he never found the time during his hectic schedule to turn his unpublished doctoral dissertation into a monograph—that is, until he was encouraged to do so upon his retirement. Few unpublished theses have been as widely recognized. As scholar Greg Marchildon said in his Introduction, "While difficult to obtain, Johnson's thesis filled such an important gap in the literature that it was actively sought out and cited in subsequent articles dealing with the Saskatchewan government during the CCF years."[7]

Johnson spent nearly five years revising the work. When it was finally published in 2004, Allan Blakeney, a former Saskatchewan premier who once worked alongside Johnson in the public service, effusively claimed that the book was "a massive contribution to understanding government in Canada ... destined to become a classic."[8]

What was most revealing, though, was the new title for the study. Reflecting on what the Douglas government had tried to achieve in Saskatchewan, now from the perspective of sixty years later, Johnson called the book *Dream No Little Dreams*. The words were just as applicable to his own public service career.

Stanley Knowles

———————————— ✄ ————————————

The pair could have been twin brothers; it was remarkable how they were identical in so many respects. Tommy Douglas and Stanley Knowles, slight in build and bespectacled, had both survived childhood illnesses. Their first jobs were in the printing business as linotype operators, a trade that paid them more than their fathers had earned in their trade. And they were both preachers, graduates of Brandon College, who stepped down from the pulpit to become socialist politicians.

But whereas Knowles was soft-spoken, more cerebral, Douglas was gregarious, often witty, and usually garnered more attention. Knowles didn't mind. He knew that their respective skills complemented one another. They became close and lifelong friends and colleagues. As he later said, "He shone in some things that I didn't and I shone in things that he didn't." [1]

Stanley Howard Knowles was born to Canadian parents in California on 18 June 1908. His father, from Nova Scotia, and his mother, from New Brunswick, had met at a Methodist prayer meeting in Boston and had been married at the Knowles home in Nova Scotia in 1904. His father, Stanley Ernest Knowles, had lost his tools—and hence his livelihood—in the San Francisco earthquake of 1906, and in desperation moved to Los Angeles to become a machinist for the street railway. [2]

During his final year at Brandon College, Stanley Knowles took turns with Tommy Douglas preaching on alternate weekends at Calvary Baptist Church in Weyburn. BRANDON UNIVERSITY ARCHIVES

Both of Stanley's older siblings had died soon after birth. Little Stanley was also sickly, until in desperation he was placed on goat's milk. When he was only ten years old, his mother succumbed to tuberculosis.[3]

By age fifteen, having skipped two grades, Stanley had his high school diploma from Manual Arts High, where he had learned the printing trade. The following year, 1924, he visited his aunt and uncle, Tom and Ida Bailey, in Carberry, Manitoba, and only reluctantly returned home to California. He wanted to live in Canada and vowed to come back within two years.

Stanley studied at the California Christian College in Los Angeles, working a night shift as a printer to support himself. He then headed back to Manitoba, and after fixing the broken linotype machine at the *Carberry News Express*, ran that newspaper for a few months. But he was anxious to continue his education and returned briefly to the United States—this time to work in a printing shop in Boston, Massachusetts—to earn sufficient money to attend Brandon College in the fall of 1927.[4]

That's where Knowles and Douglas first met. The day was 27 September 1927, and both were entering the three-year B.A. program. Tommy had already been at Brandon for three years, completing his high school credits, and Stanley would later joke that it took him only half the time to secure the same degree as Douglas.[5]

Knowles and Douglas became fast allies at Brandon.[6] When a scheduled course in socialism was cancelled, they led a student protest that got the class reinstated. And when Tommy ran for "senior stick" or student association president in his senior year, Stanley was his greatest cheerleader, leading the student body in a rendition of "Hippy Skippy."

Knowles proved the better student of the two. Upon graduation in June 1930, Stanley received the general proficiency medal, whereas his classmate Tommy was a gold medallist in debating, dramatics, and oratory.[7]

But the real contest between the two friendly rivals was played out across the border in Saskatchewan. During their final year at Brandon, while both were still students, Knowles and Douglas took turns preaching alternate weekends at Calvary Baptist Church in Weyburn. When the time came for the congregation to decide on the new minister, it chose the personable Tommy over the more scholarly Stanley.[8]

A few months later, when Tommy married Irma Dempsey in Brandon, Stanley was the best man. Knowles then went the biblical second mile on behalf of his college pal and took over the Weyburn services so that the newlyweds could honeymoon in Winnipeg. When Mr. and Mrs. Douglas finally arrived in Weyburn, Knowles had organized a welcoming reception at the railway station.[9]

Stanley Knowles also played a decisive role in Tommy Douglas's decision to enter federal politics. Tommy had run unsuccessfully as a Farmer-Labour candidate in the 1934 Saskatchewan provincial election and was happy to return to his church work, even though his supporters were urging him to contest the upcoming federal election as a candidate for the new Co-operative Commonwealth Federation Party. But he remained adamant that he was not going to run, that he had done his duty.

Then, just before the nomination meeting, the superintendent of the Baptist Church in western Canada visited Tommy. The church official had interviewed members of Douglas's Weyburn congregation and learned that most supported his recent venture into politics. At the same time, he admonished Douglas, "This is to be the last. You're not to run again." When the preacher replied that people wanted him to try for the federal seat, he was bluntly told, "Leave it … and if you don't … you'll never get another church in Canada." Douglas shot back, "You've just given the CCF a candidate."[10]

This decision, in the heat of the moment, was reinforced a few days later when Knowles, now an assistant minister in the First Baptist Church in Winnipeg,[11] wrote to ask whether Douglas was going to run in the 1935 general election. "Many of us in the church are looking to you to speak for the church in the political field," Stanley bluntly told him. "If you're asked to run, you've got to run … you just can't run away from this situation."[12] Tommy talked the matter over with Irma, and together they agreed he should seek the nomination— even if it meant being struck off the rolls of the Baptist church.

In 1958, Douglas reflected on his decision to leave the church for politics and whether the Weyburn congregation had made the right decision in choosing him over Stanley: "Later, when I became a CCF politician, some of the deacons were thinking that probably they'd made a mistake, and that they should have taken Knowles. But eventually Knowles became a CCF politician, too, and they'd have been stuck either way."[13]

Knowles stayed out of politics until 1942 when, as a federal CCF candidate, he won a by-election for the riding of Winnipeg North-Centre and replaced party founder J. S. Woodsworth. He would serve in the House of Commons for almost four decades, longer than any other CCF/NDP member of parliament, including his good friend, Tommy Douglas, who joined him on the Opposition benches in 1961 as the first leader of the New Democratic Party.

During his lengthy parliamentary career, Knowles wrote extensively on reform of the rules of the House of Commons and was reverentially known as a "walking rule book" and the "conscience of the Commons."[14] But what is sometimes lost in his story is the reason why he entered politics—the same reason that drove his classmate Douglas to do the same thing. "I finally determined," Stanley told Tommy in 1944, "that I could serve the Kingdom of God better in politics than in the pulpit."[15]

Sam Lawson

It was a memorable day for both major league baseball and Saskatchewan mental health policy. On 8 October 1956, Don Larsen, a journeyman player for the New York Yankees, pitched a 2–0 perfect game (no hits, no walks) against their cross-town rivals, the Brooklyn Dodgers. It was—and remains to this day—the only perfect game in World Series history and propelled the Yankees to yet another championship.

That same Monday, in Denver, Colorado, Dr. Sam Lawson, the new director of the Psychiatric Services Branch in the Tommy Douglas government, presented what became known as the Saskatchewan Plan to the Eighth Mental Health Institute of the American Psychiatric Association. The controversial plan called for the decentralization of mental health facilities so that patients could receive treatment within seventy-five to ninety miles of their home community.

Both events made history in their respective fields. But just as Larsen's perfect game is something that professional pitchers have since tried and failed to duplicate during the annual October classic, the Saskatchewan Plan was also never completely implemented, never fully realized. And Sam Lawson never forgave the CCF government.

Frederick Samuel Lawson was born in China in 1902 to Canadian missionary parents. Educated at a mission school in Shanghai, he

Dr. Sam Lawson presented the Saskatchewan Plan to the American Psychiatric Association at its Denver meeting in October 1956. SASKATCHEWAN ARCHIVES BOARD R-A11601

qualified in medicine at the University of Toronto in 1928. He practised general medicine in Warkworth, Ontario, from 1930 to 1936 and then did a graduate degree in psychiatry through the Ontario Hospital Service.[1]

It was during Lawson's graduate training that he no doubt met another student psychiatrist, Donald Griffith McKerracher. Not only did the pair earn the same diploma at roughly the same time, but they also both joined the Royal Canadian Army Medical Corps in 1941. As well, they shared a strong interest in community psychiatry. These coincidences would lead to an exciting opportunity at the end of the Second World War.

In late 1946, the Saskatchewan CCF government recruited McKerracher to serve as the first director of its new Psychiatric Services Branch. Premier Tommy Douglas wanted the mentally ill to receive the same quality of treatment as the physically sick and looked to his new provincial psychiatrist to modernize Saskatchewan's mental health programs. McKerracher started with the most obvious problem area—the administration and operation of the province's two large mental hospitals. He appointed Lawson superintendent of the Weyburn facility in 1947 and then transferred him to the other large hospital in North Battleford the following year.[2]

Reforms were possible in Saskatchewan because of the overwhelming desire to devise and implement a more humane way of treating mental illness. As one example, Lawson ended the practice of keeping some patients naked, others in restraints.[3]

From the premier's office down, the CCF government actively sought creative solutions that would put Saskatchewan at the forefront of mental health services and, at the same time, help reduce the public stigma commonly associated with mental disease. To this end, Lawson, McKerracher, and Dr. Humphry Osmond—the new medical superintendent at Weyburn—debated the merits of replacing larger custodial institutions with smaller community facilities, especially in a province with a predominantly rural population.[4]

This idea was not new. Since the early twentieth century, mental health advocates had been calling into question the practice of isolating patients in large hospitals, arguing that admission to these kinds of facilities was little better than incarceration and did little, if anything, to help the patient get well. The solution, for psychiatrists like Lawson, was to build smaller hospitals where patients would have greater, more frequent interaction with the local community.[5]

These informal discussions resulted in the formulation of the Saskatchewan Plan, which was grounded in the basic premise that no human being should be incarcerated in an institution when a better solution could be found. Other key principles included: that the mentally ill should have the same standard of care as the physically ill; that such care should be as easily available, with equal continuity; and that any in-patient facility should be so designed and constructed that it assists in the patient's recovery, allows for separation of patients into compatible groups, is staffed adequately, and is small enough to allow the personal approach.[6]

Lawson called on the services of architect Kiyoshi Izumi, who was working with Osmond at Weyburn, to give physical expression to these guiding principles. What Izumi devised was a "socio-petal" or circular design, which did away with corridors and effectively tried to recreate the sense of being in a small village. These small community hospitals were to be constructed in regional mental health districts, so that patients would no longer have to be admitted to the province's two large mental institutions and be forgotten. "It was not simply ... that the program was revolutionary," Izumi explained, "the buildings were revolutionary too."[7]

It was this concept, aptly dubbed the Saskatchewan Plan, which Lawson presented to the American Psychiatric Association at its Denver meeting in October 1956. Just a year earlier, Lawson had been named the new head of Saskatchewan's Psychiatric Services Branch when McKerracher became the head of psychiatry at the new University of Saskatchewan medical school, and so Lawson spoke with a certain authority. McKerracher, who had also played a role in the development of the plan, was there, too, that day. But instead of being in the audience with Izumi as Lawson presented his paper, McKerracher was in front of a television, watching Don Larsen pitch his perfect game.[8]

The Saskatchewan Plan nicely dovetailed with the call from the World Health Organization to move away from large, isolated, and overpopulated mental hospitals in favour of smaller regional facilities. But getting the CCF government to follow Lawson's lead was another matter.

Part of the problem was the architectural design. Several features of the Izumi plan went against existing building regulations and hence did not qualify for federal construction grants. And the provincial government was not prepared to build the new community hospitals without federal support. Nor was it prepared to compromise on this issue. The design consequently had to be revised several times.[9]

The other stumbling point was the cost of the plan. Starting with Swift Current in 1957, Lawson wanted the province to construct six regional mental hospitals, as well as make major structural modifications to the Weyburn and North Battleford institutions. These projects would have had a potentially ruinous effect on the provincial budget for both capital and operating expenses[10]—at a time when Saskatchewan's mental health per capita expenditures were already the highest in Canada.[11]

Lawson's single-mindedness of purpose also did not help matters. When he became director of the Psychiatric Services Branch, he used the existing wretchedness of the Weyburn and North Battleford hospitals to call for the implementation of the Saskatchewan Plan. That was the only way, Lawson told Deputy Health Minister Dr. Burns Roth, to turn things around.

Lawson was even more assertive with Walter Erb, the new minister of Health. Sensing the new minister was weak, the psychiatrist told a meeting of the Canadian Mental Health Association (CMHA) in Regina in 1957 that the well-being of mental health patients was being compromised in the province by the failure to move on the Saskatchewan Plan.[12] Such criticism from a high-ranking civil servant, from within, was not only inappropriate and unfair[13] but ran counter to the Douglas plan to begin a push toward province-wide medicare. The premier was understandably furious.[14]

The death knell of the Saskatchewan Plan was ironically delivered by Griff McKerracher. Although he initially embraced the idea of small regional psychiatric hospitals, by the end of the 1950s, McKerracher was promoting the treatment of mental health patients in psychiatric wards in general hospitals. This approach, aided by availability of new psychotropic drugs,[15] had been found to be just as effective as the supposed benefits of the Saskatchewan Plan.[16] Besides, it qualified for cost-sharing support from the federal government.[17] As a concession to the plan's proponents, however, the Douglas government went ahead with the Yorkton Psychiatric Centre in 1964.

Dr. Sam Lawson left for Ontario in 1966 to take up a position with the Workman's Compensation Board. He died four years later at the age of sixty-eight, still disillusioned with the fate of the Saskatchewan Plan.

What Lawson failed to appreciate is that the reform-minded Tommy Douglas could afford only so much reform. With the CCF government firmly focused on introducing province-wide medicare, there were limits to what was financially possible.[18] Unfortunately, the cost of the Saskatchewan Plan proved too prohibitive, too risky, even for Premier Douglas.

Hugh MacLean

He was the conscience of the convention. On 13 July 1944, just three days after Tommy Douglas was officially sworn in as Saskatchewan's first CCF premier, the provincial party held its annual convention. The delegates were in a jubilant mood—and for good reason. One month earlier, the CCF under Douglas had romped to office in one of the most lopsided victories in Saskatchewan electoral history.

But Dr. Hugh MacLean was set on realizing an even bigger achievement, an even bigger dream. In a keynote address to the convention on the state of Saskatchewan's health service, MacLean reminded the enthusiastic delegates about medicine's technical and social dichotomy. Medical science, he observed, had "progressed at an almost unbelievable and miraculous speed" but "a very large proportion of our people find it impossible to obtain these services."[1]

No one at the convention valued MacLean's comments more than Tommy Douglas. And within fifteen years, after getting the province's finances in order following the twin challenges of depression and war, the CCF premier announced in a December 1959 radio broadcast that his government would push ahead with a universal health insurance plan.

Although never fully appreciated, MacLean had much to do with the introduction of medicare in Saskatchewan. In a letter several years earlier to MacLean, Douglas humbly acknowledged, "In a sense you are the spiritual godfather of both the Medical School and the University Hospital, as well as of our general health program in the province. It was your ideas which laid the foundation for the health program which we are now carrying out."[2]

Hugh MacLean's humanitarianism and idealism were rooted in his understanding "the relationship between poverty and the neglected health of the population."[3]

Born in Glasgow, Scotland, on 30 July 1878, he immigrated with his family to Marthaville, Ontario, in 1887, where he obtained his elementary school education, while earning extra money as caretaker at his two-room school and the local Methodist church. Upon graduation from high school in nearby Petrolia, he found work as a hod carrier and then a freight handler in Winnipeg, where he also took a three-month course at Normal School (teacher's college). He taught in the hamlet of Dunrea, Manitoba, for two years, boarding with the local doctor and his wife. Despite feeling queasy while watching his first appendectomy, he decided to pursue a career in medicine.

Twenty-nine-year-old MacLean graduated from the University of Toronto Medical School in 1906. After a brief period at the Gravenhurst Sanatorium, he headed west to Lang, Saskatchewan, where he purchased a medical practice, including the equipment, horse and buggy, and cutter for winter travel. He borrowed the down payment from his fiancée, his childhood sweetheart—the daughter of the Methodist minister in Marthaville. At Lang, where he and his wife raised three daughters, he was on-call every hour of the day, every day of the year.

In 1913, MacLean did a year's residency in surgery in Chicago. On his return to his family in Lang, he sold his practice and moved to Regina, where he quickly emerged as one of the city's leading surgeons. By 1925, he had been named a Fellow of the American College of Surgeons.

MacLean never enjoyed the same success in his other passion—politics. While serving on the Regina public school board, he met Major

Dr. Hugh MacLean, a mentor to Douglas, had much to do with the introduction of medicare in Saskatchewan. SASKATCHEWAN ARCHIVES BOARD R-A3399

James Coldwell (whose first name was not a military title), a school principal and popular alderman. Both perceived that the federal government was not doing enough to solve Canada's post-war problems and embraced the new western-based National Progressive Party. MacLean even ran as the Progressive candidate for Regina in the 1921 federal election. But he failed to win the seat, while the new party swept the rest of the province and held the balance of power in Canada's first minority government.

MacLean's politics moved steadily leftward through the 1920s in response to the inequities he saw first-hand in his medical practice and in his work for the school board. And by the early 1930s and the onset of the Great Depression, he had become a convert to the moderate reform socialism espoused by his friend Coldwell and at the heart of the new Co-operative Commonwealth Federation Party. MacLean tested the political waters again in the 1935 federal election, this time as one of the CCF candidates for Regina. He placed a dismal third and forfeited his deposit, but took solace in Tommy Douglas's victory in Weyburn for the fledgling CCF. Later that same year, he was awarded the King George V medal for distinguished public service.

In December 1936, MacLean required gallbladder surgery. Brushing aside the option to go elsewhere for the operation, he chose to have it done locally and barely survived. By this point in his political career, he was serving as vice-president of the provincial CCF Party and extolling its virtues on the radio. But the botched operation had robbed him of his energy, and MacLean was forced to give up his large surgical practice. He retired in 1938 to the warmer climate of Los Angeles, California. Within a year, though, he was well enough to resume practice and soon became chief of surgery in the Santa Monica hospital.

Nor did he abandon his interest in Saskatchewan politics. Two of his three daughters lived in Regina, the other in Calgary. Every summer, MacLean and his wife would return to Canada for a prolonged stay with them and their six grandchildren. These visits enabled him to check on the fortunes of the CCF, as well as confer with Tommy Douglas, who was toying with the idea of running for the leadership of the provincial party. The two men formed a strong bond and kept up a regular correspondence. Douglas once claimed that, next to Coldwell, MacLean was his main confidant, "whose advice I valued greatly."[4]

Dr. MacLean was in Regina for the 15 July 1944 Saskatchewan provincial election when Tommy Douglas led the CCF to power and formed North America's first social-democratic government. MacLean would prove to be an influential force in the coming years. It was MacLean, for example, who persuaded his friend Douglas to assume the important Health portfolio in addition to duties as premier.[5] This decision sent a clear message about the importance of health care to the new CCF government.

At MacLean's urging, Premier Douglas introduced a number of health initiatives in his first few years in office. MacLean helped convince Douglas to commission a provincial health services survey by the renowned physician Dr. Henry Sigerist of Johns Hopkins University. MacLean's speech to the July 1944 convention served as a blueprint for the Sigerist report and, more important, its recommendations.

One expert in the area has even suggested that the famous Sigerist report "was intended merely to lend authoritative credibility to a plan conceived and promoted by a doctor he would never meet." According to Jacalyn Duffin, a professor of the History of Medicine, MacLean was nothing less than "the 'godfather' of the new health care system."[6]

There could have been no finer tribute to Dr. Hugh MacLean, who retired a second time in 1953. He died in La Jolla, California, five years later, never knowing that medicare would not only be adopted in Saskatchewan, but come to be one of the defining features of Canada.

Wendell Macleod

He was known to both friend and foe as "Saskatchewan's Red Dean." [1]
J. Wendell Macleod, the founding dean of the new five-year medical
program at the University of Saskatchewan, believed in the idea of
social medicine—that doctors should see their patients as individuals,
the product of their environment and community, and that any diagnosis and treatment should include some consideration of the world
in which patients lived. [2] This thinking found a natural home in Saskatchewan in the 1950s as the Tommy Douglas government gradually
moved toward the introduction of a province-wide system of universal
medicare. Macleod was a fervent admirer of the CCF government and
what it was attempting to do in the area of health reform under Douglas's inspired leadership.

But Saskatchewan physicians were never comfortable with a socialist as the dean of Medicine. Nor did they really appreciate Macleod's
reforms in medical education. And when Premier Douglas finally introduced his medicare plan, Saskatchewan's red dean was effectively
chased from the province by the medical community.

John Wendell Macleod was born on 2 March 1905 at Kingsbury in
the eastern townships of Quebec. The eldest of four children (all boys)
of a Presbyterian minister, Wendell was profoundly influenced by his

Douglas recruited Wendell Macleod (right) to serve as the first dean of the new medical school at the University of Saskatchewan. SASKATCHEWAN ARCHIVES BOARD R-A5724

father's dealings with the poor and disadvantaged, and came to believe in the practical application of Christianity to society's ills—what was then known as the social gospel.

Wendell attended high school and then university in Montreal. As a medical student at McGill University, his long-term goal was to become a medical missionary. But his experience as a labourer-teacher with Frontier College at a Sudbury, Ontario, mine during the summer of 1925—where workers at loose ends might spend their spare time drinking, gambling, and whoring—confirmed that there were injustices and inequities to be tackled in Canada.

Macleod graduated with his M.B., B.Ch. from McGill in 1930, winning two top prizes, the Holmes Gold Medal and the Stewart Prize. He interned at the Royal Victoria Hospital in Montreal and was a resident in internal medicine there for a year before moving to Washington University and the Barnes Hospital in St. Louis, where he specialized in gastroenterology.

While in practice in Montreal during the Great Depression, Wendell joined a study group on the unemployed led by Dr. Norman Bethune. Bethune was concerned about the deplorable health of the destitute and the paucity of medical services available to them. The group's call for some form of health insurance, however, came to naught. Macleod also attended meetings of the League for Social Reconstruction, which provided the intellectual leadership to the fledgling federal Co-operative Commonwealth Federation Party. The spirited discussions on the merits of democratic socialism with people such as F. R. Scott, King Gordon, Eugene Forsey, and Graham Spry set the stage for Wendell's later experience as Saskatchewan's red dean.[3]

Macleod enlisted in the Canadian Navy during the Second World War. Stationed in Halifax, he spent three months as the medical officer on a destroyer on convoy duty before being appointed principal doctor for the local naval hospitals. Wendell's war service earned him the O.B.E. (Officer of the Order of the British Empire). His reputation as someone who believed in medicine's responsibility to society also elicited an intriguing offer from A. M. "Sandy" Nicholson, a Saskatchewan CCF MP in Ottawa, who encouraged him to move to Saskatoon to help develop the new medical school that was being planned for the University of Saskatchewan. Macleod, though, did not regard himself as ready for such an important undertaking—he told Nicholson that "he was a better follower than a leader"[4]—and instead accepted a position with the Winnipeg Clinic at war's end.

Saskatchewan did not give up. Before Macleod even began work at the Winnipeg Clinic, Dr. Fred Mott, an advisor to the Douglas government on public health matters, invited Wendell to Regina to talk about the proposed College of Medicine. "The possibilities over the years ahead here in Saskatchewan are boundless," Mott predicted, "if we develop a university centre keyed to progressive as well as scientific thinking."[5]

The wooing continued through the late 1940s, as Mott, with Douglas's blessing, continued to send Macleod regular updates about the province's desire to establish a first-rate medical school and new university hospital in Saskatoon. Wendell, in turn, had grown disenchanted with the Winnipeg Clinic, especially its emphasis on seeing as many patients as possible, and he eventually relented.[6] In February 1951 he formally applied for the position of dean of the new medical school. Two months later, he received a simple telegram: "Appointment approved—for July 1, 1952."[7]

Wendell Macleod was named the first dean of Saskatchewan's new medical school because he was seen as a person of vision, someone who could break new ground. Still, he faced a Herculean task. Although a College of Medicine had been part of the university's plans since 1907, only a two-year pre-clinical medical school was in place by 1926. Now, it was up to Macleod to create Canada's first post-war full-degree medical school in a province that was widely regarded as a rural backwater.[8]

What made the challenge particularly attractive, though, was the "outside" support that came with his appointment. The Rockefeller Foundation was willing to pay his salary from September 1951 until July 1952, while the Commonwealth Fund in New York came to the rescue with a travel grant. While still living in Winnipeg, then, he toured medical schools in Canada, the United States, Britain, Scandinavia, and continental Europe and saw first-hand how medical education was handled by different countries.[9]

Macleod submitted his detailed plans for the medical college just one week before he officially became dean. He called for "development of a department of Social and Preventive Medicine, rural preceptorship, internship, the role of general practitioners in teaching, the integration of intern training and postgraduate instruction on a province-wide basis, and the appointment and organization of a full-time clinical teaching staff." [10] It was an ambitious blueprint, one that complemented the provincial government's own agenda in the area as set out in the Sigerist report. It also had the blessing of University President Walter P. Thompson, who confided to his diary that Macleod's appointment was "one of the very best things done for the University ... He is a man of great ability and complete integrity, personal charm, desirable social attitudes, and skill in handling men." [11]

Over the next few years, Macleod recruited faculty from across the country, the United States, and overseas. The appointment of full-time clinicians and instructors for the new school was a first for Canada. He also adopted a new medical curriculum, one that made a direct connection between social and cultural determinants and patient care. [12]

Macleod, who reportedly "[n]ever functioned in low gear," [13] thrived in his new job. But general practitioners in the city, resentful of the changes wrought by the new school and faculty, remained aloof, if not suspicious, and never really accepted him as part of the medical community. This friction between "town and gown" was tolerable as long as Macleod had the support of the university. But J. W. T. Spinks, the new president as of 1960, was no admirer and seemed determined to handcuff Macleod at every opportunity.

Macleod's situation deteriorated in 1961 when the CCF government announced that it would be introducing medicare legislation and the College of Physicians and Surgeons of Saskatchewan countered by threatening to go on strike. Macleod tried to remain on the sidelines, but when he learned in November of that year that the full-time clinicians group in the medical college supported the CPSS decision to withdraw medical services, he asked to be relieved of his duties. [14]

Wendell Macleod moved east to Ottawa where he enjoyed a distinguished career as executive secretary of the Association of Canadian Medical Colleges. [15] When he retired in 1970, he worked to raise the Canadian profile of Dr. Norman Bethune, someone who had personally shaped and informed Macleod's own career and his belief that adequate medical care should be available to all.[16]

This belief had been a defining feature of his tenure as dean of the University of Saskatchewan medical school. That's why Tommy Douglas, battling terminal cancer, made a point of attending Macleod's eightieth birthday party in Ottawa in 1985. This struggle for medicare was also raised during Macleod's farewell party in Saskatoon in January 1962. His good friend, Dr. Allan Bailey, perhaps said it best: "He always seemed ahead of us and some of us could never quite catch up."[17]

Vince Matthews

Tommy Douglas knew from the beginning of his CCF premiership that the group most likely to oppose his plan to introduce medicare was the Saskatchewan medical profession. Despite his assurances, many doctors were convinced that any compulsory scheme would put the practice of medicine under government control, and they recoiled at the prospect of becoming little more than state workers under a socialist regime.

The need to lessen, if not calm, these fears dogged Premier Douglas in the years leading up to the introduction of medicare in Saskatchewan. Ironically, though, it was a doctor—Vince Matthews—who demonstrated that the medical community's concerns were exaggerated. As medical health officer for the Swift Current Health Region #1 (SCHR), Matthews presided over a groundbreaking scheme that successfully delivered universal medical and hospital care throughout the southwest corner of the province. Douglas could not have asked for better evidence in support of his cause.

Vincent Leon Matthews was born at Kincaid, Saskatchewan, on 6 February 1922. He took his pre-medical years at the University of Saskatchewan and then graduated in medicine from the University of Toronto in 1945. His specialty was public health. Matthews was named

As medical health officer for the Swift Current Health Region #1, Vince Matthews presided over a groundbreaking scheme that successfully delivered universal medical and hospital care throughout the southwest corner of the province. PAT MATTHEWS assistant to the director of Regional Health Services in Saskatchewan in 1947. The following year, he accepted the position of medical health officer with the Swift Current Health Region. Unlike his two predecessors who lasted on the job only a few months, Matthews remained with the region for nine years and brought some much-needed stability—and in the words of an historian of health care, a "principled yet practical approach."[1]

The SCHR was Saskatchewan's first and only *regional* plan for universal health care. For just fifteen dollars per person per year (plus a property tax of 2.2 mills), the residents of the worst-hit region during the 1930s Great Depression had access to a complete range of services—from doctor care and hospitalization to children's dental and public health services. The Saskatchewan government's contribution to the experimental regional plan was a modest twenty-five cents per capita.[2]

The SCHR owed its existence to the efforts of local community leaders, who came together under Bill Burak's organizational impetus to launch their audacious health care plan. This same spirit of co-operation animated the operations of the board. Secretary-treasurer Stewart Robertson ran the district with the able assistance and advice of board chair Carl Kjorven, a farmer from near Cabri. Robertson, Wolan (the doctors' representative), and Matthews would have coffee most mornings at the Venice Café in Swift Current to deal with any difficulties as they arose, such as a new doctor over-servicing his patients. Or they would talk about ways to improve the delivery of services. This informal, open approach led to the amicable resolution of problems that might otherwise have undermined the smooth operation of the plan. As Dr. Gordon Howden (a general practitioner at Maple Creek during the 1940s[3]) explained during a CBC Radio "Ideas" program in 1990: "doctors and municipal people felt ... that it was our plan. It was a local plan, we could change things, we could communicate, there wasn't a political overtone at all ... It was a give-and-take situation with the municipalities and the doctors, both willing to learn, and being able to change the plans."[4]

Matthews also served as the SCHR accounts assessor, in addition to his duties as public health officer, and gathered statistics on all aspects of the program. When the regional plan began, covering 13,932 square miles of the most severely drought-stricken part of the province, only nineteen medical doctors serviced the area, including four specialists in Swift Current. With assured payment, and the return of doctors from overseas duty, their numbers swelled to thirty-four in 1947 and thirty-six in 1948, representing a higher doctors-to-population ratio than any other part of rural Saskatchewan.[5] This development had a domino effect. The infant mortality rate, for example, fell from a high level before 1946 to the lowest rate in Saskatchewan in 1965—14.4 per thousand births.[6]

There were other benefits. For the first time, there were hard figures for the actual cost of providing a full range of medical services—a remarkably frugal $9.83 per person per year in 1947 and $10.23 in 1948.[7] Medical doctors, moreover, were now paid cash rather than relying on payment such as chickens or sides of beef as they had experienced during the 1930s.

Despite these statistics, there still remained the matter of the doctor-patient relationship and whether the regional medical care insurance program was adversely affecting the practice of medicine. There was certainly no dispute with how Matthews conducted himself. He provided seamless integration of preventive work with medical care to a degree probably not seen anywhere in Canada before or since, and in doing so, quietly earned the respect of both the medical profession and the general public.[8]

Other doctors in the SCHR were aware that specialists in Regina and Saskatoon looked askance at this experiment in "socialized medicine." But at the same time, these doctors appreciated the special relationship that existed between themselves and the board. Dr. J. A. Matheson of Gull Lake reported in the *Saskatchewan Medical Quarterly*: "There have been times when we in the Swift Current area felt like black sheep ... We have been trying out some ideas that have not been approved." He went on to describe the benefits of the scheme: "security and stability ... better incomes ... The patients are getting a better service ... partly due to an increase in the number of physicians."[9] Dr. Cas Wolan, for his part, offered a more succinct assessment of the situation: "the Health Region trusted the doctors [and the] doctors trusted the Health Region."[10]

Interestingly, these views were echoed by outside observers. In 1946, Dr. Art Kelly, deputy secretary of the Canadian Medical Association, reported that the Swift Current regional board enjoyed a large measure of local autonomy. He characterized the region as a "successful experiment in the large-scale provision of medical care, courageously applied, efficiently managed and remarkably free from attempts to make the facts fit preconceived ideas, financial or otherwise."[11] *Maclean's* magazine also did a story on the SCHR and found that the doctors had few complaints about the plan and its operation.[12]

The Saskatchewan College of Physicians and Surgeons, however, was worried about the spread of the Swift Current medicare scheme to other areas of the province and helped to defeat the creation of similar plans in the Regina Rural and Assiniboia–Gravelbourg regions in 1955. This setback meant that the SCHR "remained a one-of-a-kind experiment."[13] But it also meant that the success of the only health plan of its kind in the province was difficult to ignore. Indeed, the SCHR gave the CCF government the confidence to go forward with universal medical care for the entire province.

On 13 October 1961, less than a month before Douglas's resignation as premier became effective, and two days after the second session of the 1961 Legislature opened, the minister of Public Health, J. Walter Erb, introduced and piloted through the Legislature the long-planned medical care insurance bill. Although the plan was to be centrally financed, it was still the government's intention to retain the Swift Current example of medicare administration on a regional basis. Douglas himself favoured this compromise, saying, "The closer you can keep an administration to the people, the better."[14] As it happened, the centralists later won out and the costs of medicare skyrocketed over the years that followed. The benefits of regional administration were also lost. No one was more aware of this mixed outcome than Vince Matthews.

In 1957, Vince Matthews moved to Regina to head the Medical and Hospital Services Branch of Saskatchewan Health. He was a member of the Thompson Advisory Committee on Medical Care, 1960–62. From 1962 to 1963, he served as acting deputy minister of Health and negotiated with the Saskatchewan Medical Association on behalf of the province during the doctors' strike.[15] Matthews completed his career as the distinguished head of the Department of Social and Preventive Medicine at the University of Saskatchewan from 1964 to 1987. He died suddenly in Saskatoon on 7 October 1988.

Matthews demonstrated the benefits that accrued when doctors co-operated with municipal administrators in the Swift Current Health Region. He gave Tommy Douglas the ammunition he needed to take on the Saskatchewan medical profession over the introduction of a compulsory, province-wide medical care plan. In a December 1959 radio broadcast announcing his government's intention to proceed with medicare, the premier told his provincial audience that the SCHR experience demonstrated that "there was nothing sinister about public medical care; the government was not threatening to put doctors on salary; a public program paying doctors did not destroy the doctor-patient relationship—nor did it scare doctors away."[16]

Fred McGuinness

It was a tall order by any stretch of the imagination. But as Premier Tommy Douglas told Yorkton newspaperman Pat O'Dwyer on a train trip back to Regina from Toronto, he knew exactly the kind of person he wanted to head up Saskatchewan's Jubilee celebrations for 1955. "I was looking for a man who was a combination of Barnum and Tchaikovsky," Douglas recounted. "I wanted somebody who could put on a first-class show, but I didn't want just entertainment … I wanted the people of Saskatchewan to have a better understanding of their own history, particularly their own local history … the part the pioneers played … I didn't want a circus, but at the same time I didn't want it so long-hair that nobody but intellectuals would take any interest in it."[1]

O'Dwyer recommended public relations consultant Fred McGuinness, who ironically was travelling on the same train. McGuinness was intrigued by the premier's ambitious plans, especially since the anniversary was still three years away,[2] and agreed to submit a Jubilee proposal. His "aggressive and imaginative responses" encapsulated the mixture of confidence and imagination that Douglas was looking for. It was readily apparent that with McGuinness at the helm, the Jubilee celebrations would "enhance the standing of the province in the eyes of provincial residents … bring the name of Saskatchewan to the attention of all Canadians and Americans [and] … promote

Fred McGuinness served as executive director of the Saskatchewan Golden Jubilee Committee.
SASKATCHEWAN ARCHIVES BOARD R-A3267-1

the name of Saskatchewan as no provincial name has been promoted before." [3]

Douglas had found his showman-artist and hired McGuinness as executive director of the Golden Jubilee Committee, asking him to assume his duties in the fall of 1952. "We wanted to get started early," the premier reasoned, "so there'd be plenty of time to plan and get the maximum amount of participation by every possible community." [4] McGuinness, for his part, shared this vision and promised Douglas that he could convince nearly a million Saskatchewan residents to join in the celebration.

Born in Brandon in January 1921, Frederick George McGuinness was only twelve years old when his father died. "It was as if a light had gone out in my life," he later confided in an interview. [5] McGuinness, formerly a good student, was now the only male in a household of seven women, his widowed mother, five sisters, and a maid. [6] Fred had to repeat grade eight and then failed grade nine twice. He quit school and got a job as a railway telegraph messenger delivering telegraphs by bicycle, but also learned Morse code from a kindly operator.

At age eighteen, McGuinness joined the Canadian navy at the start of the Second World War and served as the Morse code operator on a submarine chaser. [7] Badly injured in a naval shipwreck, he had a plaster cast from hip to toe, followed by a body brace. He spent a year in hospital, using two canes, before having surgery on his left femur at Deer Lodge Hospital in Winnipeg. Pus drained from osteomyelitis in his femur—the same disease that troubled Tommy Douglas for most of his life. [8] When McGuinness improved sufficiently, he attended St Paul's high school and then United College in Winnipeg, still supported by two canes, but able to use part-time work in telegraphy to pay his way. [9]

In 1942–43, while studying pre-med at the University of Manitoba, McGuinness was invited to become a spokesperson for war bonds—in part because of his own wartime experience, but even more so because of his commanding voice. The job was financially rewarding, at eight dollars per speech, and he spoke in offices, factories, even the pit at the Winnipeg Grain Exchange. It also convinced him that he was not meant to be a doctor and he got work with the federal government as a speech-writer before turning his hand to public relations.

When McGuinness took up his duties in Regina as executive director of the Golden Jubilee Committee, he became part of an impressive team that included Legislative Librarian John Archer,[10] secretary to the committee, and Saskatchewan Provincial Archivist Lewis Thomas. The chairman was Judge Edward Milton "Ted" Culliton, whose appointment, according to McGuinness, was a stroke of pure political genius. Whereas Douglas and the Liberal Culliton had once shared a "cobra-mongoose relationship" in the Legislature, Culliton, now as a judge of the Appeal Court of Saskatchewan, joined the committee as "one of the most respected legislators in rural Saskatchewan."[11]

It was McGuinness, though, with his infectious enthusiasm, who energized the committee and gave it direction and focus. Archer described him as "a go-getter with ideas and with the personality and drive to convert ideas into deeds."[12]

McGuiness toured the province, leaving in his wake local jubilee committees in 642 communities! The celebrations took many forms. He encouraged communities to write and publish a local history, while their pioneers were still available to tell their stories. The result, in McGuinness's words, was "that Saskatchewan's early history is better recorded than that of any other province, or so the parliamentary librarians told me."[13]

He also realized that tens of thousands of citizens had been forced to leave Saskatchewan during the drought and depression of the 1930s and consequently encouraged communities to schedule massive local homecomings for 1955. He also pushed communities to build upgrading projects, *without* provincial subsidies. These facilities of lasting value included hundreds of parks, pools, libraries, community centres, and even town halls.

Finally, there were several special projects, such as a new provincial museum, the designation of over fifty historic sites, an anthology of Saskatchewan prose and poetry,[14] a movie,[15] and a youth choir.

Nearly fifty major sporting events and national meetings were held in Saskatchewan, as well as a world-class Hereford conference and sale in Regina and an Angus cattle event in Saskatoon.[16]

Premier Tommy Douglas took an intense interest in McGuinness's activities and developed a "behind-the-scenes arrangement" to keep informed about Jubilee progress without seeming to intrude. He would invite McGuinness to his office on most Saturday afternoons, or sometimes, had both Mr. and Mrs. McGuinness to his residence for tea, muffins, and chatter on a Sunday evening.[17] Douglas even chose McGuinness as his chauffeur when he had a distant trip.

To this day, McGuinness fondly remembers the stories that Douglas used to enliven his speeches, such as when the pair attended a school opening at Oxbow: "He'd get up before an audience and say, 'A couple from Broadview that I know moved out to the West Coast and he took up golf and she took up going to auctions. And once in a while he will wake up in the middle of the night and yell, "Fore," and she will wake up and yell, "Four and a half!"'"[18]

The Jubilee celebrations were officially launched in May 1955 when Governor General Vincent Massey presided over the dedication of the new one-million-dollar Museum of Natural History in Regina. There followed some 475 local events throughout the province, many of which Premier Douglas attended as a featured guest.[19] Invariably, the achievements of the province's pioneers were the highlight of the festivities. "I remember one old man who was ninety-one," reported Douglas, "who showed me his lovely bouquet of flowers and then said with tears in his eyes, 'They haven't forgotten me.'"[20]

The closing ceremonies, broadcast over the radio, were held Labour Day weekend in Regina and featured four surviving Saskatchewan premiers. Douglas used his banquet address to remind his audience that the vision of the pioneers would serve the province well in the coming years: "The pioneers did more than build a province, they left us a heritage of courage and determination, of good neighborliness [sic], and service to one's fellow man, and qualities like that will make any province strong and prosperous."[21]

At the end of the Jubilee year, McGuinness stepped into a new career as a journalist, first with the *Medicine Hat News* and then the *Brandon Sun*. At each, he became vice-president and publisher.

McGuinness later became a regular contributor to Peter Gzowski's national radio show, "Morningside," and was renowned for bridging "the chasm between the hicks and the slicks."[22] He also had his own weekly CBC radio broadcast, "Neighbourly News," on Sunday mornings until it was cancelled in 1987 in spite of the protestations of Stanley Knowles in Parliament. McGuinness then launched a syndicated newspaper column that ran in weekly newspapers across the prairies until macular degeneration forced him to quit in 2001.[23]

One of his books, *Manitoba: The Province and the People*, won the Margaret McWilliams Medal for best history book in Manitoba for 1987. He received an Honorary LL.D. from Brandon University in 1997, the Order of Manitoba in 2002, and was made a Member of the Order of Canada in 2004.

All of these accolades spoke to McGuinness's undisputed role as "the voice of the prairies." But like his former boss Tommy Douglas, he was equally proud of his reputation as "the master of the anecdote."[24] Fred today cracks that at age eighty-nine he is in his "anecdotage."

Griff McKerracher

He wanted to convert Saskatchewan's mental hospitals from large custodial institutions to smaller treatment facilities—from an incarceration-focused model to a preventive one. And that was only the first step in making the treatment of mental health a government priority.

Griffith McKerracher, or Griff as he was known to friends and colleagues, was recruited in November 1946 to serve as Saskatchewan's new director of psychiatric services. It was his assignment to reinvigorate and transform the province's outdated mental health programs as part of the new CCF government's general overhaul of the health care system. Indeed, Premier Tommy Douglas not only had a deep interest in mental health issues from his days as a Weyburn preacher, but believed that psychiatric services were often overlooked or forgotten in any discussion of the province's health care issues.[1] He wanted Saskatchewan to be known for its enlightened policy in the area, and McKerracher to be the beacon that led the way.

Donald Griffith McKerracher was born in Chatham, Ontario, on 18 February 1909. He studied medicine at the University of Toronto but had to suspend his studies for a year to earn some money to cover his expenses. He found work as a psychologist at the Hamilton mental health clinic—a detour that put him on the path to his future career.

Griff McKerracher insisted that the main purpose of Saskatchewan's mental hospitals should be therapy and not custody. MCKERRACHER CENTRE, SASKATOON HEALTH REGION

McKerracher graduated in 1935, did a one-year internship at Vancouver's General Hospital, and then returned to the University of Toronto to specialize in psychiatry. With a diploma in hand by 1938, he held various positions within the Ontario mental health system for the next three years before enlisting in the Canadian Army. McKerracher was responsible for organizing psychiatric treatment for the war effort, first in the Toronto military district and then later as a consultant at a major neurological hospital in England.

This wartime experience, in the words of one authority, would "provide the inspiration for many of the organizational innovations [McKerracher] subsequently implemented in Saskatchewan."[2] It was needed. At the end of the Second World War, mental health patients in the province were being housed in two large "hospitals," one at North Battleford, the other in Weyburn (the largest building in the province when it opened in 1921). A third building intended for Saskatoon had to be shelved because of the Great Depression.

Tommy Douglas knew the Weyburn facility intimately and had grown to dislike it—even though it was the source of some of his jokes. He regularly gave services there in the early 1930s and later commented, half seriously, "they [the patients] would remember the sermon you had delivered and the main point of it, which was much better than most of my congregation downtown could do. And sometimes better than I could do."[3] Douglas had also stayed late one afternoon, after the staff shift-change, and was mistaken as a patient by an attendant and detained until he could prove who he said he was.

What bothered the future Saskatchewan premier about places like Weyburn was that they were little better than holding pens that offered little opportunity for meaningful treatment because of the crowded conditions and lack of trained staff. Douglas maintained that mental hospitals should be the last place to send patients, that more emphasis should be placed on prevention, and that the general public had to be educated in order to remove the stigma commonly associated with mental disease.[4] He once told the Saskatchewan Legislature: "steps should be taken ... to get at these people before they get to hospital, to provide for early diagnosis and treatment … there is no more disgrace for one member of the family to get mentally ill than there is for any other member of the family to [get] pneumonia."[5]

To justify this new policy direction, Premier Douglas commissioned Clarence M. Hincks of the National Committee for Mental Hygiene in 1945 to report on the state of the province's mental hospitals. He found both institutions to be severely overcrowded—almost double their official capacity: North Battleford housed 1,716 patients in a building intended for 1,174, while Weyburn groaned with 2,485 patients in a 1,040-bed facility. In their place, Hincks recommended what was known as "community psychiatry"—the creation of regional mental hygiene clinics and the eventual "inclusion of psychiatric services in all the general hospitals of the province."[6]

Douglas embraced these findings, especially when it was suggested that these changes would help improve public attitudes toward mental disease. As a step in this direction, the CCF government introduced a new policy providing for free psychiatric services, the first province in Canada to do so. But the premier needed someone like McKerracher, as commissioner of mental health services, to bring about the necessary changes.

It was said that Griff McKerracher "could display a laughing twinkle in one eye with the other gazing seriously into the future."[7] What this genial psychiatrist saw in Saskatchewan—or at least hoped to see in a few years—was a society where mental disease was considered an integral part of general medicine and where mental health patients would be treated in the first instance by general practitioners in their home communities rather than shuffled off to separate, impersonal mental institutions.[8]

McKerracher carried this vision forward on several fronts. First, there was the almost immediate establishment of full-time (fourteen) and part-time (sixty-three) regional mental hygiene clinics throughout the province.[9] These clinics were intended to reduce the overcrowding in the two large provincial mental institutions and, more important, reduce the trend toward hospitalization. And it worked. After the opening of a full-time clinic at Moose Jaw, for example, admissions to the Weyburn facility from that area dropped.[10]

With advice from McKerracher, the CCF government also passed a revised Mental Health Act in 1950. This legislation moved the main purpose of mental hospitals from "custody to therapy," reorganized the Division of Mental Services into the Psychiatric Services Branch, and made medical doctors, no longer the courts, responsible for deciding who should be admitted.

There were also changes at the patient care level. Employees saw their workday decreased from twelve to eight hours and their pay increased. A training program for psychiatrists, approved by the Royal College of Physicians and Surgeons, graduated five to seven psychiatrists each year.[11] Finally, McKerracher and a legal advisor from the premier's office created a new occupation—psychiatric nurse—with a training program and formation of a Psychiatric Nurses's Association. This development was another first in North America.[12]

In 1954, McKerracher was chosen as the founding professor and chair of psychiatry in the new University Hospital in Saskatoon, where he orchestrated another "quiet revolution" in both teaching and clinical practice over the next fifteen years. When the University Hospital opened in Saskatoon in 1955, psychiatric patients were treated similarly to those on medical and surgical wards. They were free to visit the cafeteria and obtain passes to visit outside the hospital. No one was restrained. McKerracher even admitted ninety unselected patients who had been committed to the North Battleford Hospital.[13] General practitioners could visit their patients and some were allowed to take part in their hospital care. McKerracher looked upon family doctors as first-line caregivers for most mental illness—an approach he liked to call his "one song."[14]

"Even if McKerracher was clinically naive, appearing to believe that mental illness would succumb to a mixture of care, sympathy, concern and trust, that naivety was more than counterbalanced by the depth and sincerity of his concern for the plight of the mentally ill.

Because he was a man of immense charm, he easily persuaded others to share his concerns." [15]

Griff McKerracher died in Saskatoon on 24 March 1970. To his medical colleagues, he was a great leader, a pioneer psychiatrist, and humanist, who was far ahead of his time.[16] Among his many honours, he was elected a Life Fellow and vice-president of the American Psychiatric Association (the latter in 1960–61), served as president of the Canadian Psychiatric Association (1955–56), and was a member of the expert advisory panel on mental health for the World Health Organization.[17]

Tommy Douglas genuinely appreciated what McKerracher had achieved in the field of psychiatric services for the province. But the premier was personally stung by McKerracher's public complaints in later years that the CCF had not gone far enough or done enough. "There is no government activity," Douglas defended his record, "which has had such a rapid increase in expenditures as the Psychiatric Branch."[18] Maybe, for a change, it was not Douglas but McKerracher who was caught up in wishful thinking.

Eleanor McKinnon

She was considered one of the ten best-dressed women in Canada in 1954. Miss Eleanor McKinnon of Regina, according to a *Leader-Post* story, had been chosen by a national magazine to represent Saskatchewan because she epitomized the "career woman at her best. Always impeccably groomed from her smoothly brushed dark hair ... to her straight seams and neatly shined shoes, Miss McKinnon manages to look the part, as well as be, the efficient secretary."[1]

Her selection probably sent a chuckle through the Saskatchewan capital—and not because the modest woman didn't deserve the honour. Rather, it was because McKinnon served as private secretary to Tommy Douglas, Saskatchewan's socialist premier. He was the one, and not McKinnon, who was usually in the spotlight.

Eleanor Madeline McKinnon really had no business working for Tommy Douglas. Born in Weyburn in 1912, she was the second daughter of Weyburn storekeeper Norman McKinnon, a rock-hard, congenital Liberal. The party connection was conferred on the McKinnon children at birth. All five siblings (Margaret, Eleanor, Keith, Ruth, and Jean) were delivered at home by Dr. Hugh Eaglesham, the future Liberal MLA for Weyburn.

Eleanor first met Tommy Douglas during her high school years in the early 1930s when she attended Calvary Baptist Church with her family. She remembered how the new preacher always took off his wristwatch and placed it on the pulpit when giving a sermon. Douglas claimed that the brain could not absorb more than the behind could stand and limited his remarks to twenty minutes. Tommy quickly gained a loyal following in Weyburn, including the McKinnon family. But their admiration for the Baptist minister never extended to embracing his radical politics, and they remained staunch Liberals.

Eleanor wanted to attend the University of Saskatchewan, but her father forced her to attend Brandon College, a Baptist college. Since tu-

Eleanor McKinnon greatly admired Douglas and the work he was doing and would have followed him anywhere. J.W. HIND

ition and board at both institutions totalled one thousand dollars, it was religion, and possibly the good train connections between Weyburn and Brandon, that influenced her father's decision. At Brandon College, discipline was tough. Bible study was held at 8.30 A.M. each Saturday. Eleanor thought her parents wanted her to be a missionary in a foreign field. Her mother was amused by the idea: "No, heaven help the heathens, if you do." [2]

After graduating with a Bachelor of Arts degree in 1933, Eleanor worked for a year in her father's store before securing a position as secretary to Dr. A. D. Campbell at the large Weyburn Mental Hospital. She loved the job—despite the fact that there were 2,485 patients in a facility designed for only 1,040—and spent almost a decade there.

That's when her former preacher, the leader of the new provincial CCF government, presented her with a quandary.

Douglas often visited the Weyburn mental hospital during his days as a local minister. And that's probably where he saw the ever-capable Eleanor in action. A few days after the 15 June 1944 election, Tommy telephoned Eleanor and offered her the position as his private secretary. "I was absolutely astonished," she later confessed.[3] Wondering why she should leave a job she really liked for the uncertainty of the unknown, Eleanor sought advice from two people. Her sister Ruth's father-in-law, said, "Take it." Her boss at the hospital was equally blunt: "I won't be here for ever."[4]

Dr. Campbell even went with Eleanor to Regina to interview Douglas about the position and told the premier that she would make an excellent secretary except for one drawback—she couldn't spell! Eleanor accepted the position at a starting salary of seventy dollars per month and never looked back.

Years later, Eleanor learned that she had been secretly investigated by the CCF caucus committee as a possible inappropriate appointment because of her Liberal family background. Nothing came of it. Working with Tommy Douglas, she was immediately converted to the CCF cause and supported the party for the rest of her life.

It's not known whether Norman McKinnon ever forgave Tommy Douglas for taking his daughter from the Liberal fold. The fault lines in the Saskatchewan political landscape were deeply ingrained. But the CCF provincial leader could not have chosen a more dedicated, more competent, more sensible assistant than he found in Eleanor McKinnon over the next four decades.

Eleanor, in a word, was unflappable. She had to be. At the premier's office, the phone rang every five minutes. "What a zoo!" she remembered.[5] Tommy breezed in each morning cheerful, always with a big smile. He had an open-door policy and tried to see everyone who came to his office. Few people made appointments.

The ever-charming Eleanor was the gatekeeper. "We never let anybody go away," she remembered, "if they had a problem."[6] But she

Eleanor McKinnon, Tommy's long-time secretary, was described as "the centre of calm in the near-chaos of the understaffed premier's office." SASKATCHEWAN ARCHIVES BOARD R-A10679-2

did stop some people she recognized as former patients of the Weyburn hospital. Tommy McLeod, who was there from the beginning as Douglas's economic advisor, described Eleanor as "the centre of calm in the near-chaos of the understaffed premier's office."[7]

Shortly after taking office, Douglas starting giving Sunday evening "Fireside Chats" over the radio. The weekly, fifteen-minute broadcasts produced an avalanche of mail. "Sometimes it would take most of the morning to open it and read it," Eleanor recounted.[8] Every letter—and there were literally hundreds—was answered. Eleanor would stay late, putting in hours of overtime, evening after evening, without any overtime pay. None was expected. No one thought of it.

She composed and typed answers to most letters, but put aside for Tommy's input those that were too difficult. Douglas read and signed the responses and usually added a personal handwritten note.

Eleanor had a simple filing system: alphabetic. There were files for Agriculture, Cancer, Hospitals, and so on. Her niece, Ellie Pattilo, recalled: "She had really high standards. Accuracy meant a lot to her … things had to be accurate and proper and right—all the things that make for an excellent secretary."[9] That included her personal appearance and how she dressed. But despite her reputation for running the premier's office with good-natured efficiency and a gentle firmness, she consistently received low pay—as did most other civil servants, especially women, working for the CCF government.

Eleanor excelled at whatever she tackled. In the late 1940s, she accompanied Douglas on a trip to northern Saskatchewan to inspect the Beaverlodge uranium mine near Lake Athabasca. A newspaper editor followed in her wake and heard a constant chorus of praise for her stamina and agility wherever he went. "Miss McKinnon breezed through this primeval country and … is rapidly becoming a legend in the northland," he later acknowledged.[10]

When Tommy was contemplating running for the national leadership of the New Democratic Party, he asked Eleanor, "If I should let my name stand would you come with me?" Without hesitation she answered, "Yes."[11] Eleanor went from the premier's outer office in the stately Saskatchewan Legislature to a dingy basement office near the airport from where Douglas ran his campaign to get elected to the House of Commons. She accepted the move with her typical grace. She greatly admired Douglas and the work he was doing and would have followed him anywhere.

Eleanor worked for Douglas in Ottawa for twenty-two years before retiring to Regina in 1983. She renewed old friendships, golfed at the Wascana Golf Club, and cheered for her beloved Saskatchewan Roughriders. Upon her death in January 2004, she was remembered in a *Leader-Post* column as the woman who unselfishly "Stayed by Premier's Side."[12] But that was not the full measure of McKinnon—just as her selection as one of Canada's best-dressed women was only one aspect of who she was.

Douglas certainly knew better and said so. About 1949, he candidly told a reporter: "She probably knows more about the government than any other person through handling so much interdepartmental business. Her work deflates the whole theory of female secretaries not making good executives." [13]

Norman McKinnon

It was not the first time that Tommy Douglas had stared defeat in the face. Nor would it be the last. Running as the CCF candidate in the Weyburn constituency in the 1935 federal election, the thirty-one-year-old Douglas faced an uphill battle against Liberal incumbent Ed Young. In the provincial election just a year earlier, local voters had sent a Liberal to the Saskatchewan Legislature. Now, in 1935, it seemed that they were prepared to deliver a similar outcome.

On election night, 14 October, the returns from the Weyburn city polls gave Douglas a disappointing 31 percent of the vote. The Liberals smelled victory and staged an impromptu victory parade led by merchant Norman McKinnon—ironically, the very person who recruited Douglas as pastor for Calvary Baptist Church in 1930. But that was politics in Saskatchewan. Party loyalty usually transcended all other considerations.[1]

In the end, though, it was the preacher who would be taking a seat in the House of Commons. When the results came in from the rural polls the next morning, Douglas ended up with 7,280 votes to Young's 6,979. To McKinnon's chagrin, a CCF victory had been snatched from the jaws of defeat.

Norman McKinnon's emphasis on children's religious education opened the way for Tommy Douglas to become the new minister at Calvary Baptist Church in Weyburn.
BOB LAMPARD

The relationship between Norman McKinnon and Tommy Douglas was full of paradoxes. The McKinnon family members were pioneer entrepreneurs and diehard Liberals. To stretch things slightly, one might even label them today as "the Sam Walton family of Saskatchewan." From a business viewpoint, they had little in common with Douglas, the first social-democratic premier in North America.

The McKinnons came from Ontario to Weyburn in 1902 and quickly built up a thriving business in southern Saskatchewan, seemingly out of a desire to outpace the growing new province.[2] What began as a modest one-storey general store was transformed by 1912 into an imposing, three-storey brick building. The McKinnon department store boasted one hundred people on its payroll and featured a meat market, soda fountain, ice cream parlour, and something new, both freight and passenger elevators. Little "cash cars" flew on wires to and from all departments to the business office on the second floor, returning with the appropriate change for the customer, who watched them with fascination. Neil, the patriarch of the family, was one-time mayor of Weyburn and later became known as "Saskatchewan's Merchant Prince."

His eldest son, Norman (born 1885), inherited the mantle. By the 1920s, the department store organized special trains to bring customers from as far away as Assiniboia. Many came for the twice-yearly fashion shows, showcasing merchandise that Norman had purchased on buying trips to eastern Canada and the United States; the models, ranging from mature women to teenagers, were accompanied by music from a live orchestra. There was also the annual McKinnon Santa Claus Parade, which handed an orange and a bag of candy to each Weyburn child. It is little wonder, then, that the McKinnons advertised, with justification, that they were "Saskatchewan's foremost store," outclassing anything in Regina, Moose Jaw, or Saskatoon.

The McKinnon family was not interested only in business. They were also deeply religious and it was through the Calvary Baptist Church that Tommy Douglas came into their lives. Neil and his spouse were among fourteen Weyburn Baptists who formed Calvary Baptist in 1906 (Neil was listed as the church's treasurer). Four years later, Norman was named one of the church's three governing deacons, a position he held for the rest of his life. He also served on the senate of Brandon College, established in 1899 to train ministers for the Baptist Church.[3]

Norman firmly believed that the spiritual work of Calvary Baptist should be centred on children's education. This philosophy was not shared by Reverend R. S. McClung, who maintained that the Sunday school should "be subordinate to the work of the Church."[4] When McClung submitted his resignation in September 1929, charging that his work as pastor was being obstructed, the congregation sided with McKinnon.

Douglas later said that he admired Norman McKinnon's "genius for religious education. He had done a great deal of work among young people and children and built up a particularly different kind of Sunday school or church school as they called it than any I've ever seen. Lots of older people attended there, but it was a young people's church."[5]

Norman McKinnon's emphasis on children's religious education opened the way for a new minister at Calvary Baptist. But how that minister was chosen was somewhat unorthodox.

Elsie McKinnon was one of Weyburn's leading women. BOB LAMPARD

In November 1929, the board of deacons reported that arrangements had been made with Brandon College to send student ministers (or "pulpit supplies") to Weyburn until the position was filled.

Dr. J. R. C. Evans, the new president at Brandon, chose his two brightest students, T. C. Douglas and Stanley Knowles, for the assignment. Over the winter, they took turns travelling to Weyburn by train to preach on alternate Sundays. After hearing each present about half a dozen sermons, the congregation voted to award the position to Douglas on 23 February 1930.

The decision did not affect the men's friendship. Even after Douglas had accepted the offer, the pair continued to preach on alternate Sundays through April. And when Douglas married Irma Dempsey that summer, Knowles was not only best man at the wedding but also returned to Weyburn to preach sermons for two Sundays while the newlyweds honeymooned in Winnipeg.

Tommy's formal ordination occurred in the Weyburn church on 15 October 1930. He could not have started his posting at a worse time. The Great Depression had ravaged Canada for the past year and showed no signs of weakening its grip on the economy.

Douglas knew that a minister's life was more than delivering sermons and that he would be expected to be a presence in the community, ready to counsel young people, visit the sick and elderly, and simply listen to anyone's troubles. But nothing prepared him for the steady traffic to the church's doors—transients looking for their next meal or local townspeople and district farmers wanting help. Even the great McKinnon store was impoverished. Groceries were moved to the basement, a bargain clothing section was added, and the third floor and part of the second were made into suites.

Nor was Tommy as minister at Calvary Baptist immune from the economic downturn. He was being paid $39 per week at the start of 1931, but then his salary was reduced to $34.50 in August and then further cut back to $31.05 in January 1934. One week, the collection was only $8.50. By the end of that year, Calvary Baptist had been forced to borrow money from the foreign missions fund just to stay afloat.[6]

By 1934, Tommy Douglas had come to embrace the Christian socialism of the new Farmer-Labour Party and decided to contest the Saskatchewan election as the candidate for Weyburn. He placed a respectable third. Dr. Hugh Eaglesham, the successful Liberal candidate, had delivered all five of Norman McKinnon's children in the McKinnon home. And Robert Stirrett Leslie, the Conservative candidate and speaker of the house in the previous Conservative/Independent coalition government of J. T. M. Anderson, 1929–34, came second. Rev. Leslie was married to the sister of Mrs. Norman McKinnon.[7]

Douglas switched to federal politics and carried the CCF banner into the October 1935 general election. This time, he was a more experienced campaigner and used his oratorical skills to his advantage, especially during a much-publicized debate with the Liberal incumbent in the arena rink in Weyburn. His performance that night before an estimated crowd of five thousand turned the campaign in his favour and he won the hotly contested battle by a slim three-hundred-vote margin.

Never in the church minutes was there any hint of Douglas's political activities. Tommy sent letters of resignation on 21 September and 19 October 1935, but the church tabled both requests until 3 November, when the letter of resignation was "taken from the table" and Douglas was asked to continue as pastor at the salary of twenty dollars per week until the end of December.[8] His congregation was sorry to lose him.

Norman McKinnon, as Calvary Baptist's longest serving deacon, probably felt the same way. Douglas was the kind of "young people's man"[9] that he wanted for the church. But McKinnon would not live to see what Tommy would do for Saskatchewan as premier. McKinnon died in a Regina hospital on his way home from his annual eastern buying trip on 6 September 1942.[10] Without him, and with increasing difficulty in obtaining merchandise due to war conditions, his wife was forced to close the store on Christmas Eve 1942, after forty years of uninterrupted service to an extremely wide community.[11] Poor Elsie McKinnon, her only son serving overseas with the Canadian Navy, was left to inform the staff that the store was bankrupt and must close.[12] Some might argue that provincial Liberal policies at the time were also bankrupt, and that's why Douglas swept to such a resounding victory in 1944.

Tommy McLeod

The unexpected job offer was made over the telephone. It was the morning after Tommy Douglas had led the Co-operative Commonwealth Federation Party (CCF) to a landslide victory in Saskatchewan, and young Tommy McLeod called his old Weyburn friend to offer his congratulations. But Douglas had other things on his mind. He had a new provincial government to get off the ground, and he wanted McLeod at his side as his advisor.

McLeod, a teacher at Brandon College, thought about it for a moment before saying yes. "That's fortunate," Douglas half-jokingly replied. "I've already wired your resignation to Dr. Evans [Brandon president]." [1]

Most people would have been shocked by such temerity. But McLeod knew that the premier-elect had a big job ahead of him—if he was going to keep his promises to the Saskatchewan electorate— and that there was no time for formal niceties. What made the job offer even more special, though, was that it was the very first appointment made by Douglas.

The position was confirmed on 12 July 1944 when Tommy McLeod was officially named economic advisor to the Executive Council. The title came with an open-ended job description. For the

Weyburn protegé Tommy McLeod had the distinction of being the first appointment made by premier-elect Tommy Douglas. SASKATCHEWAN ARCHIVES BOARD R-A5335

next eight years, McLeod did whatever Douglas asked of him, delivering much-appreciated counsel and direction in return. No one could have asked for a more trusted advisor.

Thomas Hector MacDonald McLeod's friendship with the future Saskatchewan premier began in Weyburn in 1930. But the connection
between the two families actually went back to 1910 when Douglas's
father decided that Canada offered a more promising future than
Scotland and headed to Winnipeg with one of his brothers to look for
work. The pair stayed at a boarding house operated by Mariah Finn
(coincidentally McLeod's great-grandmother) and paid for their rent
with two gold sovereigns. The coins were passed down to two moth-
erless granddaughters in the family, one of them McLeod's mother,
Ruth. She in turn presented hers to her daughter-in-law, McLeod's
wife, Beryl, who for years wore it attached to a bracelet.[2]

Tommy McLeod never heard about the gold sovereign story until
1986, just months after the death of Tommy Douglas. But he would
have appreciated its symbolic significance—how one of the gold coins
that had been used by the Douglas family to secure its future in Canada had unwittingly become a McLeod keepsake. Maybe the two men
were meant to work together. They certainly had a strong and endur-
ing relationship.

That relationship started in the fall of 1930 when twelve-year-old
Tommy McLeod was introduced to Douglas, the recently ordained
minister at Calvary Baptist Church. McLeod, an only child, took an
instant liking to the dynamic Douglas and the activities he organized
out of the church basement for the local boys—from debating to dra-
ma to boxing. The new minister, drawing upon his own childhood
experience in a Winnipeg inner-city neighbourhood, took a genuine
interest in the local boys.

But the greater influence on their friendship, and on their lives,
was the Great Depression and how it ravaged Weyburn and the sur-
rounding countryside with the twin scourges of record low wheat prices and record drought. Years later, McLeod described his hometown in
1930 as "a place of constant hope and crushed dreams."[3]

During the early 1930s, McLeod likely watched as Douglas dealt
with a steady traffic to the church's doors: transients looking for their
next meal or local townspeople or district farmers needing some
help. He also listened to Sunday sermons that increasingly adopted a

sharp reformist edge in response to the worsening poverty and sense of hopelessness. It was painfully apparent that the church was making little headway in the crisis, even though the congregation, under Douglas's direction, was doing everything humanly possible to alleviate the suffering. Something was terribly wrong with Canada's economic system.

Douglas began to reach out to like-minded people in search of a new way of doing things. These meetings, involving teachers, labour leaders, and farmers, were often held in McLeod's father's print shop—what was known as "a sort of wind tunnel for local politics."[4] Some members of Weyburn's hot stove league wanted more government planning, others outright government ownership.

Both Douglas and young Tommy McLeod came to embrace the Christian socialism being advocated by the new provincial Farmer-Labour Party (FLP), the forerunner to the CCF. It essentially combined the practical teachings of the Bible with gradual, social democratic reform. And when Douglas ran as a CCF candidate in the 1935 federal election, McLeod, now seventeen, was at his side, helping run the campaign in Weyburn.

Douglas and McLeod remained in contact even after the Baptist preacher went to Ottawa to sit in the House of Commons as one of only seven CCF MPs. It was probably at Douglas's urging that McLeod did his undergraduate degree at Brandon College. After graduating with distinction, he earned his master's degree at Indiana University and then returned to Brandon in 1941 to teach economics.

At McLeod's invitation, Douglas regularly visited Brandon College to give seminars and debate the issues of the day. But not everyone was pleased with Douglas's presence on campus, and the dean had to field calls complaining about his "spreading of Communist propaganda."[5] McLeod steadfastly defended his friend's right to be there, especially since Douglas was himself a Brandon College alumnus.

In June 1944, when Douglas led the provincial CCF Party into the Saskatchewan election, he turned to McLeod to serve as an organizer for the Weyburn riding. Douglas was in great demand to speak throughout the province, and he needed someone to help ensure that he won his home riding. That favour was returned when Douglas made his job offer the morning after the election.

McLeod's challenge as economic advisor was essentially to help turn CCF dreams into reality. As Premier Douglas asserted in his first throne speech, the new provincial government would "create a government organization sufficient in scope to meet the needs of post-war society."[6] But that was not possible in 1944. Departments operated out of their own silos without much thought to long-term planning. As McLeod recalled, "They inherited a government machinery almost totally incapable, in terms of its organization and personnel, of meeting demands made inevitable by the kind of governing that matched their philosophy and that they intended to provide."[7]

It was McLeod who largely initiated the revolution in how the Saskatchewan government and bureaucracy would henceforth operate. Guided by the principles of interdepartmental planning and budget co-ordination, he introduced a system of organization whereby the Cabinet had a comprehensive understanding of government plans and priorities and what they could cost over several years.

McLeod brought about this change by wearing many hats. When, on 8 September 1944, the government established the Health Survey Planning Commission and appointed famed Dr. Henry Sigerist as its commissioner, a key behind-the-scenes mover was McLeod. When the new Economic Advisory and Planning Board was formed on New Year's Eve, 1945, with the newly arrived George Cadbury as its chair, McLeod was named secretary. Nearly two years later, in November 1946, McLeod "fathered" the new Budget Bureau, the first of its kind in Canada.[8] In 1950, McLeod became deputy provincial treasurer and the Budget Bureau became a branch of the Treasury Department itself.

What was truly amazing about this government transformation is that McLeod somehow found time to improve his own skills and training. Late in the first term of the Douglas government, the Treasury Board had approved an unusually enlightened leave program whereby civil servants could upgrade their education on the understanding that they would return to the employ of the government. McLeod chose to go to Harvard University and obtained his master's degree in public administration and his Ph.D. in economics.

Tommy McLeod left the Douglas government in 1952 to become the dean of Commerce at the University of Saskatchewan. Eight years later, he was named dean of Arts and vice-principal of the new Regina campus of the University of Saskatchewan, the forerunner of the University of Regina. In 1971, he joined the senior ranks of the Canadian International Development Agency to help sort out administrative problems in countries that included Turkey, Iran, Nigeria, and Botswana. McLeod retired to Victoria in 1997 and died there on 1 January 2008.[9]

It was while working in Ottawa that McLeod had his last meeting with Douglas. In February 1986, he visited the gravely ill Douglas in his apartment. Even though the former Saskatchewan premier was only days from death, McLeod recalled, "He was cheerful as ever. We talked about all sorts of things."[10] It's too bad that neither one of them at the time knew the story about the gold sovereigns.

Arthur Morton

It was the second time in two years that his electric hotplate had been found burning in his office in the Agriculture Building (later known as the Administration Building and then the College Building). And it could have been a disaster not only for his research but also for the University of Saskatchewan.

Professor A. S. Morton of the Department of History had spent nearly a decade collecting documents and painstakingly making notes for his monumental history of western Canada. But one Saturday evening in March 1927, the business manager for the university found the lights on and the stove burning in Morton's paper-filled office, right next to the university library.[1]

The calamity averted, Morton eventually published his book, *A History of the Canadian West to 1870–71*[2] in 1939. The real irony of the episode, though, is that Morton went on to play a fundamental role in the establishment of the Saskatchewan Archives Board. When the new Tommy Douglas government looked to preserve the province's documentary heritage, Morton had already done most of the groundwork.

Arthur Silver Morton was born in the small village of Iere in Trinidad on 16 May 1870. The son of Presbyterian missionaries, he studied at the University of Edinburgh, where he earned both the M.A. and

Arthur Morton in the University of Saskatchewan Library, Agriculture Building.
UNIVERSITY OF SASKATCHEWAN ARCHIVES A874

Bachelor of Divinity degrees. He came to Canada in 1896 and served as a minister for eight years before embarking on a teaching career in church history, first at Pine Hill College, Halifax, and later at Knox College in Toronto.

In 1914, at the age of forty-four, Morton was hired by the fledgling University of Saskatchewan and expected to wear two hats—one as librarian, the other as head of the Department of History. He discharged both duties admirably.

Morton built up the university library "from literally nothing to a collection of 60,000 volumes … He bought wisely on limited funds."[3] One of his greatest purchases—at a remarkably low price—was the Adam Shortt collection of Canadiana, which included the library of Sir Sandford Fleming, the first Canadian Pacific Railway chief engineer and inventor of standard time.[4] During his Saskatchewan career, Morton became known as the "unofficial keeper of the soul of the university."[5]

He was also an inspiring teacher who sought to engage students with the discipline. These efforts included the formation of an historical association three years after his arrival on campus. "His learning," his peers remembered, "was set forth as a well-ordered feast to which was added the relish of wit and anecdote. He took infinite pains with individual students winning their lasting affection and respect."[6]

It was in the areas of research and outreach, however, that Morton's contributions extended beyond the university to the wider provincial community.[7] Indeed, in coming west to Saskatoon in 1914, he shifted his scholarly interest from church history to the history of western Canada, especially the period before Canada's acquisition of the North-West in 1870. This new research focus grew out of Morton's interest in the region's history and a certain obligation to learn more about the history of his new home. But in studying Saskatchewan's past, Morton became acutely aware of the need to acquire and preserve the documentary record so that the province's history was neither forgotten nor lost.[8]

This need for a Saskatchewan archives dated back to the 1890s when legislators became concerned about the fate of territorial records. It resurfaced again in 1905 with the creation of Saskatchewan as a province. Nothing was done, though, until 1920 when the government passed a statute providing for the retention or disposal of old government records. But because the legislation was silent about the creation of a provincial archives, it actually had the opposite effect. Large quantities of government records could now be legally destroyed because there was no space to store them in Regina.[9]

Morton became vitally involved in the question because of his study of the western Canadian fur trade. He spent the better part of his summers, away from Saskatoon, doing research into the records at the Public Archives in Ottawa. In 1933, he had also been granted access to the voluminous Hudson's Bay Company Archives in London. This experience confirmed for Morton the importance of primary documents for historical study. He believed that all records should be preserved, "for we cannot know today what is valuable and what is not. The future only can settle that."[10]

In September 1936, with the backing of University President Walter Murray, Professor Morton made a personal appeal to the Saskatchewan premier and minister of education for the creation of a provincial archives. He warned that future generations "will charge us with betraying our trust if we cast away... material" instead of preserving it in an archival institution. This time, the government was receptive to the idea—but probably only because the university was willing to provide the space and an archivist, as well as cover the operating costs.[11]

In April 1937, the Historical Public Records Office was officially set up on the University of Saskatchewan campus in a basement room in one of the residences, Saskatchewan Hall. Morton got a new title too—Keeper of the Public Records. The following year, the first set of territorial government records was transferred from Regina to Saskatoon, and Morton set to work cataloguing them and preparing calendars (known today as finding aids).

By 1941, the collection was so large that it had to be relocated to the School for the Deaf. But the shortage of storage space was only going to get worse because of Morton's acceptance of the Saskatchewan land records of the former federal Department of the Interior; it was estimated that this collection would require three thousand linear feet of shelving.[12] The other problem was that the Historical Public Records Office had no legislative basis. It was simply an informal arrangement between the government and the university. There was no governing body deciding policy or overseeing the operation of the archives.

Something had to be done to put the management of the collection on a more permanent basis. After all, thanks to Morton's efforts, the records had effectively become the provincial archives. But would the new CCF government of Tommy Douglas do the right thing and pass the appropriate legislation? Morton certainly hoped so, and in late 1944, he publicly called for an archives act.

Douglas, for his part, did not have to be convinced of the necessity of a Saskatchewan Archives. When he assumed the premiership, he found that the outgoing Liberal administration had "emptied the files of almost every document that might help the CCF govern the province," including the documents for an upcoming dominion-provincial conference.[13] Douglas complained to former premier Patterson that this "act of pillage" was "most improper." Patterson lamely replied that he was only following "practices established by custom."[14]

Douglas was determined to put an end to this practice and instructed his minister of Reconstruction and Rehabilitation to work with Morton in developing archives legislation. The history professor was delighted with the news. But he would not live to see the passage of the Archives Act in the spring legislative session. He died of a heart attack during a meeting with the university president on the morning of 26 January 1945.

Premier Tommy Douglas is often credited with the creation of the Saskatchewan Archives Board. But in this particular case, it was Professor A. S. Morton who led the way and the CCF government that followed.

The Archives Act now prohibited the destruction of any public document except on the recommendation of the provincial archivist. It also expanded the acquisitions policy to include all kinds of documentary material on Saskatchewan history. Most important, though, it continued the tradition, started by Morton, of having an archives office on the University of Saskatchewan campus, whereby researchers could have direct access to primary sources.[15]

George Simpson of the Department of History reflected on what the pending creation of the Saskatchewan Archives Board meant to his deceased colleague. "To him," Simpson observed five days after Morton's death, "it was a sort of crowning to his life's ambition that provincial historical studies be placed on a sound and permanent basis."[16] Tommy Douglas would have been among the first to thank him.

Fred Mott

It was a promise he felt personally bound to keep. In the spring of 1946, Premier Tommy Douglas, doubling as his own Health minister in the Saskatchewan CCF government, introduced the Hospital Services Act in the Saskatchewan Legislature. A key feature of the legislation was a province-wide, compulsory hospital insurance plan to be in place by 1 January 1947.

But the team Douglas had assembled to oversee the implementation of the scheme, including Dr. Fred Mott, the former deputy surgeon general of the United States, did not think it could be ready in time to meet the premier's declared deadline. And they tried to tell him at a special meeting in which they asked for a twelve-month extension. Douglas, however, waved aside their arguments and told the planners to come up with a hospitalization plan—or he would find others to do it.[1]

"I told the people from the beginning," Douglas later recounted, "that we'll be making some mistakes because we're blazing a new trail, but one mistake that we will not make is the mistake of doing nothing. So we're going to start."[2]

Frederick Dodge Mott was born at Wooster, Ohio, on 3 August 1904. He grew up in a family dedicated to human welfare. His father, missionary John R. Mott, a leading figure in the YMCA, had won the Nobel Prize for his efforts in pursuit of world peace. Fred was imbued with the same spirit and spent several months in his teens as his father's secretary in Europe and the Far East.

Mott graduated from Princeton University with an honours degree in History and then entered McGill University medical school intent on becoming a family doctor. However, when sickness forced him to reconsider his specialty, his idealism took him to the wider field of rural health and medical care. There had always been work to be done in this area, but the problems had become particularly acute during the Great Depression. Mott consequently spent the better part of the next decade, after graduation in 1932, conducting medical care and public health activities amongst low-income farmers and migratory workers throughout the United States. This was followed by a posting as a commissioned officer in the U.S. Public Health Service during the Second World War.

Mott's expertise in the provision of medical care to rural populations did not go unnoticed. When the Saskatchewan government was looking for someone to head the Health Services Planning Commission, Dr. Henry Sigerist, the man who had been instrumental in the establishment of the new body, told Douglas that Mott was "the ablest man on the continent" for the job.[3] He would need to be.

Although Douglas wanted to introduce a medical care insurance plan in Saskatchewan, he knew from the beginning of his tenure as CCF premier that such a plan would probably be years away, especially given the cost to the provincial treasury. "We thought we should start with hospitalization," he observed. "We didn't feel then ... that you can set up a complete health insurance programme covering every aspect of health services all at once."[4]

Despite this initial caution, though, Douglas was still prepared to go against the advice of his own planners. When Henry Sigerist recommended in the fall of 1944 that the province introduce free hospitalization, he warned the government that it should move gradually and cover only maternity cases at first. Those on the inside agreed. Not only was the CCF government about to embark on a costly hospital-

Premier Tommy Douglas accepts his Saskatchewan hospital insurance plan card, while an understandably satisfied Dr. Fred Mott looks on (seated far right). SASKATCHEWAN ARCHIVES BOARD R-A3256

building program but also the public service did not have any experience with insurance programs.

The premier, however, was willing to take the gamble and went
ahead with his promise in the Legislature to have a provincial hospitalization plan in place by the start of 1947. He was genuinely worried that the longer the CCF government delayed the introduction of
the scheme, the greater the opposition would become. Douglas also

looked upon the plan as a crucial step on the road to medicare. As he once explained, "You get your machinery established … you get it running smoothly, and you move onto the next [step]."[5]

At the same time, though, the premier realized that his planning team needed additional expert help to meet the deadline—and save his political reputation. Douglas set his sights on Fred Mott and flew to Washington to woo the American doctor to Regina. He told Mott that he shared his father's social gospel philosophy. He also played upon the time Mott had spent in Montreal as a medical student. But what won Mott over in the end was not the famous Douglas charm, but rather the fact that Mott was married to Marjorie Heeney, the daughter of the minister of St. Luke's Anglican Church in Winnipeg. It was Marjorie who convinced Fred to accept the premier's offer.[6]

Fred Mott was named chairman of the Saskatchewan Health Services Planning Commission in the summer of 1946, a position he held for five years. A man of action and great personal integrity, he was ideally suited for the task at hand. But he also agreed with the other planners—that Douglas was being unrealistic in wanting a hospital insurance plan in place by the end of the year—and pleaded with his new boss for more time. That's when Mott was introduced to another side of Douglas.

Effectively told by the premier that there *would* be a scheme in place by 1 January 1947, Mott and his planning team redoubled their efforts. One observer claimed the situation was reminiscent of mobilization at the start of the war in 1939.[7] The staff certainly "worked under battlefield conditions—their office was an old retail store, their desks were plywood panels on trestles, and their filing cabinets were cardboard boxes on the floor."[8] All citizens had to be manually registered for a hospitalization card; there were no computers to help with this process.

Mott was at the forefront of this feverish activity. With no template to follow, breaking new territory against all odds, and with less than six months' preparation, he worked incredibly hard to meet the premier's deadline. Getting the universal hospitalization plan up and running was a testament to Mott's competency, his administrative skills, but above all, his innate ability to see the entire field of play.

But then, in early December, the plan threatened to be stillborn when leaders of the Saskatchewan Hospital Association told Douglas that they refused to co-operate with any CCF plan to take over the province's hospitals, many of which had been built as community projects. The premier assured the hospital directors that the government had no desire to manage their institutions, just pay the costs of hospitalization. As Douglas bluntly put it, he had no time "to keep track of every bed-pan."[9]

With this crisis averted, the scheme was launched on schedule on 1 January 1947. Mott and several other officials gathered at the premier's home on New Year's Eve, and as midnight approached, headed to Regina's General Hospital to witness the first patient to be admitted under the new Saskatchewan Hospital Plan.

The plan was an immediate success. For a modest annual hospital premium, families no longer had to pay for in-patient hospital services. Doctors, on the other hand, no longer had to worry about the cost of admitting patients to hospitals. As one commentator noted, "The plan became popular before it became expensive."[10] That said, there was no other scheme like it in North America, making it "one of the 'banner' firsts of the Douglas government."[11]

Fred Mott's next major assignment was chairing the Saskatchewan Health Survey from 1949 to 1951. He also served briefly as Saskatchewan's deputy minister of Health and as Canada's representative to the World Health Organization in 1951 before the United Mine Workers of America came calling. He returned to the United States to set up a network of ten regional hospitals to provide health services to half-a-million people in the coal-mining communities of Kentucky, Virginia, and West Virginia. He capped his career at the University of Toronto as a professor of medical care administration (1968–72) before retiring to Pittsford, New York, where he died in 1981.

Mott was recognized with an honorary Doctor of Laws from the University of Saskatchewan in 1955. "To him," the citation read, "we owe much of the unique accomplishment in public health and medical care planning for which this province has some renown ... he is a [pioneer] on behalf of better health services for people who need them."[12] What could also have been said is that Fred Mott enabled Tommy Douglas to keep his promise to the people of Saskatchewan.

Humphry Osmond

It was a drug that helped define the 1960s: d-lysergic acid diethyl-amide, more popularly known as LSD, or by its slang name, acid. It was synonymous with long-haired hippies, electric guitar-infused rock music, and the counterculture—all wrapped up in the phrase, "turn on, tune in, drop out," coined by self-styled "consciousness expansion" guru Timothy Leary.

But like other recreational drugs that have migrated from the laboratory to the street or living room, LSD was first used for me-dicinal purposes. The most important testing ground for the drug in the 1950s was the Weyburn mental hospital in southeastern Saskatch-ewan, where psychiatrist Dr. Humphry Osmond conducted LSD ex-periments to determine whether psychoses, such as schizophrenia, had a biochemical basis. This research was never secretive nor peripheral, but well publicized and well funded, thanks to the wholehearted sup-port of Premier Tommy Douglas. LSD offered the promise of using pills to treat mental illness, and the CCF government wanted to be at the forefront of any therapeutic breakthrough, especially if it meant the possible de-institutionalization of hundreds of patients who were otherwise languishing in places like Weyburn.[1]

Humphry Osmond was born in Surrey on 1 July 1917 in an England sapped by three years of world war. He tried his hand at writing plays, then banking, before taking up medicine. Humphry graduated from Guy's Hospital Medical School in 1942—in the midst of another war—and served as surgeon lieutenant on a Royal Navy cruiser providing convoy escort on the North Atlantic. This experience at sea introduced him to the psychological side of war and, with encouragement from a senior doctor, he decided to specialize in psychiatry.

At war's end, Osmond worked in the psychiatric unit at St. George's Hospital in London, where he and fellow doctor John Smythies found that mescaline-induced hallucinations in volunteers closely mimicked the symptoms of schizophrenia. It did not take much of a leap for the pair to conclude that the mental disease probably resulted from a chemical imbalance in the body—a hypothesis they put forward in the first publication that advanced a biochemical explanation for schizophrenia.[2]

In early 1951, Osmond and Smythies decided to launch a major investigation of the biochemical and psychological basis of schizophrenia. Their research program called for human subjects to ingest the hallucinogens mescaline and LSD so that their reactions could be monitored and collected. As Osmond later explained: "Schizophrenics are lonely because they cannot let their fellows know what is happening to them and so lose the thread of social support. LSD-25, used as a psychotomimetic, allows us to study these problems of communication from the inside and learn how to devise better methods of helping the sick."[3]

St. George's Hospital, however, had no interest in sponsoring the experiment. Osmond consequently began casting about for an institution or a place that might be willing to support his research. The timing could not have been more opportune—for both him and the Saskatchewan CCF government.

Humphry and Jane Osmond and their family arrived in Weyburn in October 1951. The city, a major service centre on a CPR branch line running southeastward from Regina, had a population of just over

Dr. Humphry Osmond conducted government-supported testing of LSD at the Weyburn mental hospital in the 1950s. SASKATCHEWAN ARCHIVES BOARD R-A11559-3

seven thousand—a far cry from cosmopolitan London. But what Weyburn offered Osmond, as the new clinical director of the local mental hospital (and later medical superintendent), was unqualified support for his research and, in the words of a former colleague, a "professional freedom for experimentation not found elsewhere."[4]

This dynamic atmosphere was largely attributable to Saskatchewan Premier Tommy Douglas, who was determined to initiate reforms on the mental health front while trying to bring about a new public understanding of mental illness. It was also actively promoted by Dr. Griff McKerracher, Saskatchewan's director of psychiatric services, who had been recruited by the CCF government five years earlier to encourage and facilitate psychiatric research in the province. Indeed, the more cutting-edge the research, the higher the enthusiasm. As one journalist neatly summed up the Weyburn scene at the time: "It was an age of bold experiments … it dared to explore the brain, the psyche and dimensions that passeth all understanding."[5]

Osmond quickly befriended Abram Hoffer, a Saskatchewan-born psychiatrist who had, only in July of the previous year, been hired by McKerracher to develop a research program in psychiatry. The pair shared an interest in the biochemical basis of mental illness, as opposed to the more traditional approach of psychoanalysis, and decided that experimentation using LSD offered the possibility of a medical breakthrough. This prospect tantalized the CCF government, and McKerracher was able to report that the province was willing to provide the start-up funds for the research.[6]

Osmond initially self-experimented with the drug. How did it affect the body, especially perception? Soon Hoffer, other doctors, their wives, nurses, and colleagues were participating in LSD experiments. Osmond described it as "'madness-mimicking'… The research on LSD was time- and culture-bound due to the drugs' short-lived legal status; it also represented a style of daring experimentation that suited the medical mores of the contemporary culture of hope."[7] Osmond even travelled to Los Angeles in the spring of 1953 to administer mescaline to author Aldous Huxley, who was intrigued by the medical trials going on in Weyburn. Huxley later recounted his experience in the book,

The Doors of Perception, while Osmond came up with the term "psychedelic" to describe how the drug brought about "an enlargement and expansion of the mind." Osmond had written to Huxley: "To fall in Hell or soar Angelic/You'll need a pinch of psychedelic."[8]

By the mid-1950s, psychedelic psychiatry was in full swing in Weyburn. Osmond's research had "transformed the hospital by attracting distinguished researchers from both academic and service disciplines to an institution that had been regarded by some as a backwater."[9] Osmond and his research team became increasingly confident, based on their studies, that "schizophrenia was a biochemical illness that produced a primary disturbance in perception."[10] Perhaps alcoholism, too, had biochemical roots. In a long-term, twenty-four-patient study of alcoholics treated with LSD, six achieved complete abstinence from alcohol throughout the long follow-up period.[11] Tommy Douglas applauded Osmond and Hoffer's innovation and encouraged communities to consider alcoholism as a medical disease. More so in Saskatchewan than anywhere else, LSD treatment of alcoholism became a regular option as "a matter of local pride and personal triumph."[12]

This research, in turn, cultivated a sense of pride in the professionals involved, a belief that they were part of something special. Kay Parley, a student psychiatric nurse at Weyburn, couldn't "think of a more exciting place to be ... than Dr. Humphry Osmond's mental hospital."[13] She explained in her reminiscences: "Practically overnight ... the hospital set about bringing itself out of the Middle Ages and into the twentieth century. During the fifties, we watched remodeling, replacement of obsolete equipment, and a general face-lifting, coupled by an awakening of attitudes and a strong emphasis on research. Dr. Osmond was not only humanitarian, he was creative, and the year finally arrived [1957] when our hospital was named the most improved mental hospital in North America."[14]

By the early 1960s, however, the psychedelic research in Weyburn started to unravel. Osmond left in 1961 to become director of the Bureau of Research in Neurology and Psychiatry at the New Jersey Psychiatric Institute in Princeton. Hoffer moved on six years later.

Their departures coincided with questions about whether LSD really had any therapeutic benefits, especially given the growing popularity of the drug for recreational purposes. Still, a 1965 article in the *New York Times* described "the experiments in Saskatchewan as good, safe examples of LSD use in medical experimentation."[15]

Humphry Osmond ended his career in 1992 as a professor of psychology at the University of Alabama in Birmingham. When he died twelve years later—of cardiac arrhythmia on 6 February 2004[16]—he was still advocating the medical possibilities of LSD and lamenting the criminalization of the drug.

It was this open-ended search for answers that had enticed Robert Sommer to come from Kansas as the first research psychologist at the mental hospital in Weyburn.[17] Sommer fondly remembered Osmond as "a roman candle of new ideas ... the most creative person I ever worked with ... most everything Humphry did was novel, for that was the way his mind worked."[18] He also deeply appreciated how the support of the Tommy Douglas government helped make Weyburn "one of the most intellectually exciting places in the mental health landscape ... [it] came very close to being ... an experimenting society ... a questioning community."[19] The after-dinner get-togethers have certainly never been the same.

Stewart Robertson

It seemed as if the whole province was watching, but one person probably more closely than anyone else—Saskatchewan Premier Tommy Douglas. In January 1947, the new Swift Current Health Region #1 (SCHR) passed a groundbreaking resolution at its first meeting: that a comprehensive medical care insurance plan be adopted as soon as possible. The same organizational meeting selected Stewart Robertson as secretary-treasurer.

It was Robertson's job to see that this experiment in compulsory, prepaid health services functioned on a day-to-day basis without any major glitches. It was no small assignment, even if Robertson did not carry a big title. Such an ambitious undertaking had never been attempted before in North America. Many people consequently regarded it as the first real test of the CCF government's plan to establish medicare in Saskatchewan in the near future. As the *Toronto Star Weekly* aptly observed, "On all sides one hears the plan referred to as an experiment, and so it is."[1]

Stewart Robertson was born in Calder, Scotland, on 22 July 1900. He was schooled in Scotland and then served with the Gordon Highlanders in the First World War. At twenty and a veteran, he moved to one of the worst possible places to seek a livelihood—on the drought-

Stewart Robertson served as secretary-treasurer for the Swift Current Health Region #1.
LEAH ROBERTSON KOLDINGNES

stricken north side of the Saskatchewan-Montana boundary. He tried farming, but his seeded grain sprouts were eaten by hordes of grasshoppers in the withering heat. The poor harvests prompted a mass exodus from the region. For the first time in provincial history, the number of farms actually declined between 1921 and 1926. But Robertson stuck it out.

In 1927, Robertson married Agnes Hanlon and took over the general store in the tiny hamlet of Loomis, almost due south of Eastend, Saskatchewan. By the early 1930s, his customers had no money to pay their bills; in desperation, this frugal Scot with a growing family accepted a job as the secretary-treasurer of the Rural Municipality (RM) of Reno in the hamlet of Vidora, along the southeastern edge of the Cypress Hills. There, Robertson found himself acting more as a relief agent than as a manager of nonexistent tax finances. It became his job to hand out apples from Ontario and codfish from the Maritimes to the starving farm families. This work was so depressing that when a similar job opened in a municipality farther north, on the other side of the hills, where occasional rain showers provided enough moisture to raise a few bushels of wheat, he began work at the RM of Webb on 1 July 1940.[2]

Robertson's new RM was "a very well run municipality, financially well managed, and a model for others … the minutes of each and every meeting were posted in the office for all to read."[3] But even then, the cost of health care proved prohibitive for most people. "Many residents incurred medical bills they could not pay," Robertson recounted, "and as the RM was being held responsible for their accounts in 1942–43, the council decided it would be logical to provide the medical services for everyone rather than pay individual bills."[4] The first municipal vote, however, was defeated because of the general fear of higher taxes. Robertson and the council persisted and presented two bylaws—one for a hospital plan, the other for a medical plan—to a municipal vote on 31 March 1944. This time, both measures were overwhelmingly approved,[5] and Robertson found himself overseeing two medical insurance plans as part of his RM duties.[6] One of the first things he did was train a local girl, Pat Ditner (later Cammer), to be his secretary.

Robertson's soft-spoken, calm demeanour served him well in his new duties. Nothing flustered him. This is probably why, two years later, he beat out ten other applicants for the position of secretary-treasurer at the organizational meeting for the Swift Current Health Region #1. The new health district had committed itself to providing the people of the southwest corner of the province with complete health services at public expense. And it needed someone with Robertson's integrity, grassroots experience, and thoughtful pragmatism to make it work.

Although technically secretary-treasurer to the SCHR board, Stewart Robertson effectively functioned as a chief executive officer for the next twenty-one years. One of his major worries was financial. It was decided from the beginning that the plan would be funded 25 percent from property taxes and the other 75 percent from personal taxes. The Saskatchewan government, in the meantime, pitched in and paid for the region's office staff, which consisted of a medical health officer, seven public health nurses, a health educator, and three sanitary inspectors.

Robertson was determined to get full value for every dollar expended. He led by example. His office was squirrelled away in the old Sykes building in Swift Current. To describe it as small was charitable. Pat Ditner, his secretary who followed him from Webb, remembered the room having "bare wood floors, no drapes on the windows, second-hand furniture and equipment [one small regulation teacher's desk, two chairs, and a coat rack] and an antiquated radiator that blew every so often, drenching everyone and everything."[7] At first, Ditner shared the same office with Robertson, but could not get much work done because of the constant interruptions. She moved to the adjacent room and was summoned by a buzzer whenever she was needed.

Ditner would later describe her boss as "a very caring, kind, even-tempered, compassionate, patient man; hard-working and willing to help when and where he could."[8] These qualities were in great demand, especially during the first few years when the SCHR faced several crises, in particular a polio epidemic in 1947 that nearly drove the plan into bankruptcy. The SCHR was saved when the hospital portion of its budget (42 percent) was assumed by the new, province-wide Saskatchewan Hospitalization plan.[9] It also owed much of its financial stability to Robertson's shrewd management. The costs of running the SCHR plan were modest, if not thrifty, especially when compared to the hundreds of millions of dollars spent on health care in the province today.[10]

This careful regard for the financial bottom line did not mean the Swift Current region received second-rate service. From a public health viewpoint, for example, the district went from being one of the riskiest places to live, to one of the healthiest. Frank Peters, senior health inspector, oversaw safe water supplies, pasteurization of perishable foods, modernization of slaughterhouses, and higher standards of sanitation in restaurants and in the modern beverage rooms that replaced beer parlours. Most towns and villages also developed municipal waterworks and sewage systems.[11]

Robertson consistently maintained that the SCHR was successful because of the regional approach to the provision of health care. It may have been financially supported by the Saskatchewan government, but the fact that it was initiated and run locally provided a sense of ownership, a sense of empowerment, but most of all, a sense of satisfaction in seeing people's medical needs met.[12] Robertson delivered this message to the provincial Advisory Committee on Medical Care in 1961. Any new Saskatchewan-wide health plan, he insisted in his brief, should be based on the SCHR model. A centrally administered program would never do. There should be "as little [control] as the provincial government can possibly get by with," he told the committee, "in order to satisfy themselves that the money is being wisely spent."[13]

The Douglas government certainly appreciated this perspective. An internal interdepartmental document revealed that the cabinet believed that the SCHR scheme was popular because of the "preservation of local creativity and responsiveness to local needs."[14] But the cabinet also did not want to create separate, regional medicare plans that might end up in competition with one another. The CCF government consequently eschewed the Swift Current model in favour of a single, uniform plan for the entire province.

Stewart Robertson retired from the SCHR at the end of 1966, but did not quit working. An avid golfer, he turned his organizational skills to the Swift Current golf course, tending to the fairways, planting trees, installing a watering system, and building grass greens. In his later years, he remained active with senior citizens' groups up until his death in March 1981.

Under Robertson's guidance, Swift Current Health Region #1 was thoroughly tested. It was made to work. Robertson provided careful management and fiscal efficiencies at a level never to be achieved elsewhere in the province. It is no exaggeration to suggest that had the experiment not been successful, "Saskatchewan's path toward medicare would have been longer and even more turbulent." [15]

Tommy Shoyama

--- ✄ ---

He was looking for a fresh start in a place where his Japanese ancestry would not be an issue. And he found it in Regina in the Saskatchewan public service.

In 1946, thirty-year-old Tommy Shoyama was hired as a research economist for the newly established Economic Advisory and Planning Board (EAPB). It was his job, along with several other experts, to advise the Tommy Douglas government on how best to direct future economic policy. This initiative was more than a simple matter of bringing about some diversification in a province that relied too much on agriculture for its economic well-being. Having run on the motto of "Humanity First" in the 1944 election, the new CCF government was committed to providing the province's citizens with equal access to the highest possible levels of education, health care, and welfare. The stumbling block was to find a way to make this reform program financially possible.

Tommy Shoyama, as someone who had been interned during the Second World War because of his race, welcomed the challenge. Within a year of his arrival in Regina, it was apparent that he had made the right decision when the Saskatchewan Legislature passed the first Bill of Rights in Canada, which prohibited discrimination on racial and religious grounds. For several years now, he had been an advocate for toleration and acceptance of difference.

Born in Kamloops, British Columbia, in 1916, Thomas Kunito Shoyama left for university in 1934 with no more than a bicycle, ten dollars, and a small bundle of clothes. He graduated from the University of British Columbia four years later with two degrees—one in economics, the other in commerce.

In 1939, Shoyama became editor of *The New Canadian*, a weekly Vancouver-based newspaper devoted to promoting the civil rights of the Canadian-born, English-speaking Nisei (second generation). This purpose would be severely tested after the bombing of Pearl Harbor in December 1941 and the subsequent forced evacuation of all people of Japanese ancestry, Canadian or otherwise, from the Pacific coast.

Shoyama was relocated in 1942 to Kaslo in the British Columbia interior, where he continued to produce *The New Canadian* as a source of information about internees and camp life. It was the only Japanese-Canadian newspaper that government officials sanctioned during the war, and Shoyama took advantage of every opportunity to question his people's enemy-alien status and to call for understanding.

"This tragic conflict," he wrote in an editorial shortly after Canada declared war on Japan, "must not destroy our hopes and aspirations to walk with honour and with dignity and with equality as Canadians among Canadians."[1] He made a similar appeal when censors threatened to shut down the paper in 1944.

At the end of the war, Shoyama served briefly with the Canadian Army Intelligence Corps. He still faced, though, an uncertain future, especially given the persistent doubts about the loyalty of Japanese-Canadians. A good friend, George Tamaki, encouraged him to seek work with the new Douglas government in Regina. He did and went on to serve the province for eighteen years.

Tommy Shoyama had the good fortune to work from the beginning with the two advisors that Premier Tommy Douglas had hand-

Economist Tommy Shoyama, who had been relocated to the British Columbia interior during the Second World War, found work with the new Douglas government.

Tommy Shoyama (standing far left) with staff members of the Economic Advisory and Planning Board. Chair George Cadbury is standing at the back, third from left.
SASKATCHEWAN ARCHIVES BOARD R-A8840

picked to help the fledgling CCF government realize its goals: Tommy McLeod, economic advisor to the cabinet, and George Cadbury, head of the Economic and Advisory Planning Board. But it was Al Johnson who would be Shoyama's closest colleague. The two acted in tandem for the better part of their Saskatchewan public service careers. It was almost impossible to mention one without referring to the other.

Shoyama, in his capacity as research economist for the EAPB, handled several tasks, including developing an administrative framework for Saskatchewan's crown corporations and devising ways to promote development of the province's natural resources. Beginning in 1950, however, he assumed a more prominent role in government economic planning when he was named secretary to the influential EAPB. Such an appointment would have been impossible only five years earlier.

Over the next decade and into the 1960s, Shoyama worked closely with Deputy Treasurer Al Johnson to ensure that government planning and the budgetary process went hand-in-hand. To this end, Shoyama sat in on Treasury Board deliberations, while Johnson attended EAPB meetings. Each brought his own specialty to the discussions: Shoyama the economic aspect, Johnson the social side.

This collaborative approach was needed most when Premier Douglas announced during the April 1959 Birch Hills by-election that his government would introduce a universal and comprehensive medical insurance plan. It fell to Tommy Shoyama and Al Johnson, as representatives of the Cabinet Committee on Planning and Budgeting, to make it happen—something that has been largely overlooked today. As a December 2006 *Globe and Mail* article noted, "While premiers Douglas and Lloyd [Douglas's successor as CCF premier] were at the forefront of the political battle, Mr. Johnson and Mr. Shoyama were constantly occupied behind the scenes in committee work and drafting of legislation."[2]

Douglas fully recognized that Shoyama and Johnson were part of "the best personnel of any provincial government in Canada."[3] The premier freely admitted that Shoyama could easily land a better-paying job elsewhere. But it was what the CCF government was trying to do that kept Shoyama in Saskatchewan. As Douglas observed, he was "not the sort of guy you can con—and he won't fall for a sob story. Yet he's got a good deal of compassion for other people's problems."[4]

There were times, though, when the premier tired of the technical jargon in the reports that were prepared for his consideration. One day in exasperation, he showed Shoyama and Johnson a letter that had been written by an irate Saskatchewan Power Corporation customer. There was only one sentence: "Some bugger bust my fence." "There it is," said Douglas. "Subject, 'bugger,' verb, 'bust,' object, 'fence.' Why can't you fellows write like that?"[5]

Such criticism was rare. By the time that Douglas had been elected leader of the federal New Democratic Party, Shoyama was his most trusted confidant. It was only natural, then, when Douglas took to the road during the winter of 1961–62 to drum up support for the new party that Shoyama was at his side. He did whatever was asked of him, including serving chicken soup to Douglas whenever he fell ill.

Tommy Shoyama joined the Saskatchewan civil service diaspora when the Ross Thatcher Liberals came to power in the province in 1964. He quickly found employment as a senior research economist with the newly formed Economic Council of Canada in Ottawa. Four years later, he became assistant deputy minister of Finance, then deputy minister of Energy, Mines, and Resources, and finally, deputy minister of Finance.

Shoyama retired from the federal public service in 1979 and returned to the west coast where he joined the public administration faculty at the University of Victoria. His many contributions to governance in Canada were not forgotten. He was awarded Officer of the Order of Canada (1978), the Outstanding Achievement Award in the Public Service of Canada (1978), and the Vanier Medal in Public Administration (1982). The universities of British Columbia and Windsor each presented him with an LL.D. *(honoris causa)* degree. He also received the Order of the Sacred Treasure from the government of Japan (1992).

Perhaps the greatest honour came in June 2007, six months after his death, when the universities of Regina and Saskatchewan established the Johnson-Shoyama Graduate School of Public Policy.

Morris Shumiatcher

In June 2003, the Saskatchewan Department of Justice formally charged David Ahenakew with promoting hatred. The former president of the Saskatchewan Federation of Indian Nations and a well-known Cree elder had made some disturbing anti-Semitic remarks to a Saskatoon reporter, even going as far as to justify the Holocaust.[1]

What was sadly ironic about the shameful episode is that it was a Jewish lawyer, Morris Shumiatcher, working for the Tommy Douglas CCF government, who had authored the Saskatchewan Bill of Rights more than half a century earlier. Shumiatcher not only shared the premier's desire to protect fundamental freedoms in Saskatchewan, but also worked to advance the rights of the province's First Nations population.

Morris Cyril Shumiatcher, the son of middle-class Polish Jews, was born in Calgary in September 1917. His father had earned a law degree after immigrating to Alberta, while his mother had studied at the University of Warsaw. Morris graduated with a Bachelor of Arts from the University of Alberta in 1940 and initially planned to do graduate work in English literature. But anti-Semitic remarks by a professor about his proposed career choice steered Morris into law. "Shumiatcher was aware of discrimination," one author has commented, "and intended to use his legal training to combat it." [2]

Morris earned his Bachelor of Laws degree from Alberta in 1941 and then continued his studies in the master's program at the University of Toronto, where he also worked part-time for the Canadian Jewish Congress, collecting information on anti-discrimination legislation. His graduate work was interrupted by the Second World War and a two-year stint (1943–45) in the Royal Canadian Air Force as a gunner. Upon his return to the University of Toronto, he secured the first doctorate in jurisprudence ever offered in Canada. By sheer coincidence, his 1945 classmates (in the future Supreme Court Chief Justice Bora Laskin's constitutional law seminar) included George Tamaki and Al Johnson, who were both hired by the new Tommy Douglas government in Saskatchewan. [3]

Shumiatcher would also be invited to Regina. Even though the new Saskatchewan premier had many talents, legal expertise was not among them. And he needed someone with a specialization in labour and related issues. Douglas consequently hired Shumiatcher to serve as legal advisor to the Executive Council. [4]

The twenty-eight-year-old lawyer welcomed the opportunity to take part in what was being hailed as the great Saskatchewan experiment. A week before the June 1944 provincial election, he had told his parents that a CCF victory could "lay the foundations for a better society ... more interested in the welfare of the human beings of the country, than in the ledgers and profits of monopolistic enterprise." [5]

Shumiatcher, or "Shumy" as he was popularly known, worked for the CCF administration for only a few years. But despite his short tenure—not to mention his diminutive size—he cast a long shadow. Besides being one of Douglas's most trusted confidants, he also served as cabinet secretary and recorded all cabinet decisions. And when the Economic Advisory and Planning Board was established, he and Tommy McLeod were appointed as advisors. Like many other senior public servants at the time, Shumiatcher did whatever was needed. That included, according to McLeod, "acting as pro-tem chauffeur for the

Morris Shumiatcher, or "Shumy" as he was popularly known, drafted the 1948 Saskatchewan Bill of Rights. SASKATCHEWAN ARCHIVES BOARD R-B2580

premier [Douglas was a notoriously bad driver], cooling out an irate taxpayer, or preparing a brief for the government."[6]

Shumiatcher's greatest contribution, however, was pushing for and then drafting a Saskatchewan Bill of Rights—something that

Douglas and the new CCF government had set as one of its key goals. During the 1919 Winnipeg General Strike, the fourteen-year-old Tommy had watched from a rooftop as armed mounties on horse-back used their guns to break up a protest parade. Douglas witnessed more police violence during his years as minister at Weyburn's Calvary Baptist Church. In September 1931, the mounted police confronted striking coal miners in Estevan and killed three men and wounded several others, including local citizens, in the ensuing battle. Then, on Dominion Day 1935, Tommy was visiting Regina when the RCMP provoked a riot by forcibly arresting the leaders of the On-to-Ottawa Trek at a peaceful downtown rally. His old friend Dr. Hugh MacLean told him how he had spent hours extracting bullets from wounded trekkers.[7]

Douglas had been equally troubled by events in Europe. In the summer of 1936, now as a CCF member of Parliament, he visited Nuremberg and watched in horror as German dictator Adolf Hitler presided over a parade of tanks and guns from the growing Nazi war machine. Douglas returned to Canada consumed by the sense of peril that Hitler posed to the world.

These experiences helped shape and inform Douglas's commitment to a pluralistic, tolerant Canada and the civil liberties that went along with it. Indeed, the 1944 CCF provincial election motto, "Humanity First," was not an empty slogan.[8] The new Saskatchewan premier was determined to use his influence and intervention to bring about a better world. At his first dominion-provincial conference in 1945, for example, he proposed the protection of "certain fundamental religious, racial, and civil liberties in a Bill of Rights [entrenched in the BNA Act]."[9] When the other premiers balked at the idea, the stage was set for Saskatchewan to take the lead.

Shumiatcher, who had been calling for human rights legislation since his arrival in Regina, took up the challenge of drafting the Saskatchewan Bill of Rights. He enlisted assistance from his many friends in Jewish socialist organizations, who, although small in number, formed "the most influential non-Anglo-Celtic group within the CCF."[10] He also benefited from the research of the Jewish Labour

Committee (JLC), which fought against anti-Semitism and promoted human rights in Canada, and from Samuel Bronfman, president of the Canadian Jewish Congress.[11] Shumiatcher not only sought to safeguard fundamental freedoms and equality rights, but promote them as well.

The Saskatchewan Bill of Rights was a remarkable piece of legislation for the time, if only because of the protection extended to racial and religious minorities.[12] Attorney General J. W. Corman even suggested it was "perhaps the most important bill that ever came before this house ... in importance, it will rank with the British North America Act."[13] The Opposition vehemently disagreed and attacked the compulsory features of the legislation, suggesting that it was more in keeping with a communist regime. But in the end, no one wanted to be seen to be opposed to such fundamental principles, and the bill passed unanimously in the spring of 1947—one year before the United Nations General Assembly adopted the "Universal Declaration of Human Rights."

Since then, some analysts have dismissed the Saskatchewan Bill of Rights as somewhat ineffectual, in part because its potential benefits were not fully tested in the courts as Shumiatcher had hoped. Instead, the CCF government preferred education, persuasion, and conciliation over prosecution.[14] Only three cases were tried under the bill's provisions and only one of them related to protection of minority rights; not one related to aboriginal rights.[15]

But there is little doubt that the discussion engendered by the provincial bill "helped to prepare the ground for the federal bill of rights in 1960."[16] One expert claims that the Saskatchewan Bill of Rights "was, and continues to be, unique ... [It] broke new ground in Canada as it protected civil libertarian values. And to this day it is the only legislation to extend this protection from abuse by powerful private institutions and persons ... Extending the reach of this protection from abuse at the hands of private institutions and persons flows from the CCF philosophy that the individual is vulnerable to abuse at the hands of corporations and other powerful private actors, not just at the hands of the state."[17]

As for Morris Shumiatcher, he continued his trail-blazing ways. In 1948, at age thirty-one, he was appointed the youngest King's Counsel in the Commonwealth. He also played a pivotal role in the formation of the Union of Saskatchewan Indians, the forerunner of the Federation of Saskatchewan Indian Nations. After he entered private practice in 1949, he spent more than forty years arguing important cases, especially constitutional matters, before the British Judicial Committee of the Privy Council and the Supreme Court of Canada. He remained a tireless advocate in pursuit of human rights and civil liberties until he died in September 2004.[18]

Henry Sigerist

It was probably one of the few times that Tommy Douglas surprised even himself. Just one day after leading the CCF Party to victory in the June 1944 Saskatchewan election, the new premier called Dr. Henry Sigerist, professor of the history of medicine at Johns Hopkins University in Baltimore, Maryland, and asked him to head a special commission to survey health services in the province. Sigerist accepted at once. According to the doctor's diary entry for that day, he was won over by "the possibility of organizing medical services in a sensible way." [1]

But the premier's offer also came with a catch—he would gladly cover Sigerist's expenses, but provide no pay. "I think he was so astonished," Douglas later recalled, "that anyone would have the gall to ask him, and then to tell him that we couldn't pay anything except his expenses, that he came." [2]

Henry Sigerist was born in Paris in April 1891 to Swiss parents. He studied classical and oriental languages before completing a medical degree at the University of Zurich in 1917 and then served briefly as a doctor in the Swiss Army. Sigerist's passion was the history of medicine, an interest he pursued as an independent scholar at the University of Leipzig's prestigious Institute of the History of Medicine.

Dr. Henry Sigerist conducted a systematic examination of Saskatchewan's health care needs.
ALAN MASON CHESNEY MEDICAL ARCHIVES, JOHNS HOPKINS MEDICAL INSTITUTIONS

In 1932, Sigerist assumed the directorship of the new Institute of the History of Medicine at Johns Hopkins University and quickly turned it into the leading centre for the history of medicine in North America. One of his initiatives included the 1933 founding of the scholarly journal, *Bulletin of the Institute of the History of Medicine* (later *Bulletin of the History of Medicine*). But it was in his role as a writer and lecturer that he made headlines.

Sigerist was deeply troubled by the apparent collapse of capitalism during the Great Depression and looked to socialism as the answer. He created a national stir in 1937 when he published a book lauding state medicine in the Soviet Union. Sigerist delighted in the controversy and used every opportunity to call for some form of compulsory health insurance. He even appeared on the cover of *Time* magazine in January 1939 and was identified in the accompanying article as the foremost American authority on health policy.

Given Sigerist's public profile—and his views on health insurance—it was only natural that he came to the attention of Tommy Douglas. While the future Saskatchewan premier was still serving as a member of Parliament in Ottawa, Sigerist had appeared before a House of Commons committee in 1943 and pushed for a greater government role in public health matters.

This approach certainly applied to the Saskatchewan situation once the CCF assumed power after the 1944 provincial election and Douglas personally took on the Health portfolio. The new CCF premier wanted to conduct a systematic examination of the province's health-care needs before embarking on any new policy initiatives. He consequently proposed the creation of a Saskatchewan Health Services Survey Commission and looked to his good friend and CCF activist, Dr. Hugh MacLean, to serve. Instead, MacLean recommended Sigerist as commission chair. That's when Douglas picked up the telephone and offered him the job.

Since then, the wisdom of Douglas's selection has been questioned. Although Sigerist was "a physician of international reputation," observed one medical historian, "there was a great deal of criticism later that a professor of the history of medicine … had been chosen rather than an expert in health services organization and administration."[3] Sigerist, however, knew exactly what Premier Douglas was trying to achieve, and equally important, why he was being enlisted for the task. "The CCF is determined to make a demonstration of what a socialist government can achieve," he confessed to his diary, "They find that the health care field is most suited because the people are aware of the problem and ready for a plan."[4]

Henry Sigerist arrived in Regina by train at 7.20 P.M on 6 September 1944. Welcomed at the station by the premier and one of his advisors—in Sigerist's words, "idealists with a realistic approach"[5]—he immediately began work the next morning. Over the next two weeks, the six-member commission travelled by car throughout the province, holding public hearings in community halls and receiving briefs from various interested groups. Sigerist found the tour "extraordinarily interesting and informative. We could feel the pulse of the province."[6] He particularly enjoyed listening to the views of farmers on what should be done. He was not so effusive, though, about his encounters with the prairie outhouse and told Douglas that he was surprised that people did not suffer from chronic constipation.[7]

Sigerist set to work on his report the last week of September and completed it at five minutes after midnight on 1 October. He privately confided to his diary that it was "the best I could do" under the circumstances.[8] Sigerist formally presented his findings to Douglas on 4 October and then departed the following morning. Even though he had spent only one month in the province, the doctor claimed that the experience would "always mean a bright spot in my career."[9]

The Sigerist report was decidedly succinct—there were only six broad themes or recommendations. But despite its brevity, it was long on ambition. The report called for the gradual implementation of "complete medical services to all the people of the Province, irrespective of their economic status, and irrespective of whether they live in town or country."[10] This goal effectively became the blueprint for medical care in Saskatchewan for the next half-century.[11]

To ensure that every citizen had access to medical care, Sigerist recommended that the province be divided into health regions for preventive medicine and curative services, each centred on a district hospital and equipped with an x-ray machine, medical laboratory, and an ambulance. He also proposed the introduction of a government-operated hospital insurance plan, which he estimated would require another one thousand to fifteen hundred hospital beds in Saskatchewan, including a new five-hundred-bed university hospital attached to a new medical college at the University of Saskatchewan. And he advocated school dental clinics, improved pre- and post-natal care, programs for the mentally ill, and health care for pensioners and widows. Many of these recommendations were quickly implemented.

It is easy, in hindsight, to dismiss the Sigerist report as well-meaning but short-sighted.[12] The proposed decentralization of health services suited the Saskatchewan of the 1930s, but offered little in the way of forward-planning for the 1950s and 1960s. But even Tommy Douglas did not foresee how post-war changes in agricultural technology would accelerate rural depopulation. He was more concerned with finding the funds to put the plan into action. Still, it did not stop the premier from introducing legislation that fall, the Health Services Act, which embraced the recommendations of the Sigerist report.

Henry Sigerist retired from Johns Hopkins in 1947 and, with the financial help of the Rockefeller Foundation, worked on his proposed multi-volume history of medicine. But he had published only one volume at the time of his death in Switzerland ten years later.

Sigerist is usually remembered as one of the world's foremost historians of science. But it was in Saskatchewan where "his message about the need for progress in both social and technical medicine [has] been understood and implemented … The sparsely populated prairie province [was] the only place on earth genuinely striving for, if not attaining, the elusive balance … His role was that of a distinguished outsider, a well-chosen catalyst who lent authoritative credibility and political detachment to a course of action."[13]

Charlie Smith

In January 2000, *Maclean's* magazine carried a feature article about Canadians who had made a difference in the twentieth century. Naturally, Tommy Douglas was on the list. But readers may have been surprised when Shirley Douglas suggested that her father's greatest achievement as Saskatchewan premier was rural electrification and not medicare. That's how her father saw it, too. "Once, when he was flying over Saskatchewan," Shirley recounted, "someone asked him what is the greatest thing you feel you have done for this province? He said, 'Look down. Right there. The twinkling lights.'"[1]

Tommy Douglas certainly deserves credit for bringing electricity to rural Saskatchewan. After all, he promised to do so in the 1944 provincial election and, despite doubts even from members of his own party, kept the promise in the 1950s. But the "unquestioned father of rural electrification" was Charlie Smith.[2] As Saskatchewan Power's farm electrification superintendent, he tackled the monumental task with an unshakeable faith in what Douglas and his CCF government were trying to do for a province that lagged behind the new Canada of the 1950s.

Rural electrification may have been part of the CCF's ambitious reform plan for post-war Saskatchewan, but it was the irrepressible Smith who literally got the poles in the ground, the lines strung, and the lights on. One author has called Smith the "mahatma of the miracle."[3]

Charles Eugene Smith was born in Oskaloosa, Iowa, on 10 March 1911. He grew up in the Swift Current area, first on a farm northeast of town and later in the town itself.[4] In 1928, the Smith family moved to the landmark Goodwin House (now restored as a provincial historic site) on the south side of Saskatchewan Landing, where Charlie's father ran a small store and market garden and his mother served as postmistress. Charlie took grade 12 by correspondence so that he could help out on the little farm known locally for its watermelons and strawberries.

In 1930, twenty-year-old Charlie joined the Saskatchewan Power Commission (Sask-Power). He started work in the Swift Current Power Plant and by the end of the decade had

Charlie Smith made the Rural Electrification Act a reality in the 1950s. DEANNA WATERS

become a company supervisor. He served in the Maple Creek, Watrous, and Tisdale districts before being brought to Regina in 1949 to turn into reality the February 1947 Rural Electrification Act.

It was a formidable challenge, even if Smith was working from a government-sponsored master plan developed by David Cass-Beggs of the University of Toronto. A post-war survey by a special provincial reconstruction council found that only three hundred farms in the province had electrical service from existing transmission lines. Saskatchewan had the dubious distinction of having the lowest percentage of farms with electric lights in the country (4.9 percent).[5]

This lack of electricity meant that rural women had to make

do without a number of labour-saving domestic devices enjoyed by their urban counterparts, and effectively sentenced them to a life of drudgery on the farm.[6] And while Saskatchewan cities were awash with artificial light at night, it was dark in the countryside, seemingly part of another world. People in the countryside had to contend with dimly lit halls and schoolhouses, especially in winter. Sports such as hockey and curling also had to be played during daylight hours. Then, there was the absence of electric streetlights, store signs, or even electric refrigeration in small-town cafes. It is not an exaggeration to suggest that the restriction of electricity to urban areas helped create two Saskatchewans by the mid-twentieth century—one with power, the other without.

In 1949, under Charlie Smith's supervision, the Saskatchewan Power Corporation conducted a test program to see if it could provide service to twelve hundred farms. Although the corporation fell short of its target by fifty-eight farms, the Douglas government announced in 1950 that it would provide electricity to fifty thousand farms and all towns and villages by the end of the decade.[7]

Many observers scoffed at the idea because of the immensity of the task: potential customers were scattered over great distances, and the main power lines initially followed road allowances "on the square." It was estimated that there would be only 1.18 farms per mile of power line, including sometimes long tap-offs (the distance from the line to the farmstead).[8] The other potential difficulty was that wheat farmers were not large consumers of electricity and their unstable incomes might make them reluctant to sign up for power, especially when they had to pay for the line and the poles to their farms.[9] Mixed farmers with livestock had a greater need for electricity. Because of the prosperity that the provincial economy was enjoying, the CCF government guaranteed the loans that allowed SaskPower to purchase an average of one hundred thousand power poles per year, together with the expensive transformers and power lines.

Smith tackled the rural electrification program with military-like organization. Construction crews, numbering around twenty men, would normally spend from four to six weeks in a particular district. In heavily wooded areas, such as the region north of Yorkton, SaskPower engaged local farmers to help clear brush and build the distribution system. This self-help program, as it was called, allowed districts to obtain power, especially in the wet year of 1954. It was also the kind of made-in-Saskatchewan solution that ensured that the construction work went smoothly.[10] Smith believed that the "major turning point in rural electrification" had been reached at the end of the 1951 season.[11] He predicted that in four years, "more miles of line [would be] built than in all the preceding twenty-five years."[12]

The arrival of a SaskPower construction crew in a district was a much-anticipated event. Rural residents often invited crewmembers to take part in baseball games and curling bonspiels—and romances. One construction foreman reported three weddings between crewmembers and local women in one year. Workers were also honoured guests at "lights on" parties. At Wawota in December 1953, local residents and SaskPower personnel were treated to a special musical program featuring the community band, choirs, and, of course, speeches by local dignitaries.[13] It was as if rural Saskatchewan had crossed the threshold from one era to another.

There was resistance, though. Some rural residents had never seen an electrical appliance in operation, while others were afraid of electricity. To ease these concerns, SaskPower created a home services division and hired Lillian Vigrass, the first of several "Penny Powers"[14] to tour the province in a van equipped with appliances, giving practical demonstrations. At the same time, agricultural engineers taught the farmer how to use electricity efficiently in the farmyard, while SaskPower distributed a booklet and offered classes on home wiring.[15] Most of the first purchases were for the farmhouse—usually a refrigerator, ending decades of trying to keep food fresh in an icebox. To encourage the consumption of electricity, SaskPower used the twin slogans, "Live Better Electrically" and "Farm Better Electrically."[16]

By 1956, all towns and villages in southern Saskatchewan were served with power. Two years later, SaskPower reached its target of fifty thousand farms. By the end of the decade, SaskPower had erected

50,300 miles of rural line at a total cost of 47.5 million dollars (of which 25 million had been paid by farmers). The cost to a farm family averaged about five hundred dollars.[17]

Charlie Smith helped usher in a revolution in rural Saskatchewan. Not only were homes more comfortable, cleaner, and brighter, but the burden placed on farm women eased, especially in food preparation and preservation and the constant hauling of water and wood.

Farmers also quickly learned the value of power to their operations, whether it be new tools, such as welding equipment, drills, and saws, or something as simple as lighting their shed or yard to extend the working hours. Large-scale dairying (with milking machines) or the poultry industry (with heated sheds) became possible for the first time. Electricity also energized local businesses—from signs to store windows to inside lighting. Children no longer complained about dimly lit rural schools, while sporting and cultural activities were no longer restricted to daylight hours.[18]

Perhaps Ted Turner, former president of the Saskatchewan Wheat Pool and later chancellor of the University of Saskatchewan, best captured what electricity meant to rural folk. "On July 31, 1952, we pulled a chain in the house and light came on," he fondly remembered that day on his Maymont-area farm. "To me that was one of the highlights of my life. Just like that, our whole lifestyle flipped over."[19]

David Smith

———— ✖ ————

It was not supposed to be part of the Saskatchewan CCF government's agenda. According to a January 1946 internal document prepared for the Douglas cabinet, the powerful Economic and Advisory Planning Board recommended that cultural initiatives "must occupy a lowly place in the general plan" relative to other, more urgent funding priorities.[1] But just two years later, the lieutenant-governor signed an order-in-council establishing the Saskatchewan Arts Board. It was the first agency of its kind in North America.

The credit for the Saskatchewan Arts Board—probably the Douglas government's most heralded cultural initiative—often goes to the premier and his minister of education and successor, Woodrow Lloyd. These two politicians, according to many accounts, collectively had the imagination and determination to see that the agency was created.

That may be true, but it was a senior civil servant who actually came up with the idea for the arts board and helped draft the terms of reference. David Smith, the director of Adult Education in the Saskatchewan Department of Education, already had the initiative in mind when he was invited west in 1946 to join the Tommy Douglas administration.[2] And he used the opportunity presented in Saskatchewan to apply what he had learned in Ontario as director of the Community Life Training Institute to push for the arts board.

David Smith pushed for the creation of the Saskatchewan Arts Board, the first cultural agency of its kind in North America. THE SASKATCHEWAN BULLETIN, APRIL 1952

David Charlton Smith was born in Hamilton, Ontario, in 1906 and raised in a strict Presbyterian household where the Old Testament and the word of God were paramount. David's mother wanted him to devote his life to the church. In fact, his parents insisted that he "not be engaged in any kind of activity other than work which was manifestly useful and serving the good of people."[3] That meant the ministry, medicine, or teaching. He decided that teaching was best for him.

David graduated from Hamilton's normal school in 1924 and worked for one year in a one-room school. He then entered the University of Toronto and secured both his B.A. and M.A. in philosophy.

He also got married—a prairie girl from a Moose Jaw railway family. The western connection grew stronger when he was hired to teach English and history at Regina College during the worst years of the Great Depression.

Smith returned to Ontario in 1936 and two years later was named director of the Community Life Training Institute in Simcoe County—a rural extension service that employed group dynamics to liberate people from traditional constraints and help them develop their own community-based organizations and services. This experiment in adult education was a resounding success. "We could hardly keep up with the demands made on us," Smith recounted. "We were running just to catch up."[4]

Smith was given the chance to bring this experience to Saskatchewan in 1946 when the Tommy Douglas government came calling for a new head of its Adult Education Division. David Lewis, national secretary of the federal CCF party, knew of Smith's innovative educational work and recommended him for the job.[5]

Smith, a self-described socialist, readily accepted the offer. Saskatchewan, at the time, served as a kind of mecca for social activists like himself who wanted to be part of the broad reform program underway. But more than that, he shared the core values of the Douglas government and its attempt to create, in his words, a "genuinely democratic society, a cooperative commonwealth."[6] For Smith, the creative force in society was found at the grassroots level. "We need to restore," he once observed, "more decision-making to local areas, the communities, where people understand and can deal with the issues."[7] This philosophy would be a central feature of the future arts board.

Forty-year-old David Smith tackled his new duties in Saskatchewan with a kind of missionary zeal. He established adult education programs in schools and generally did whatever he could to bring about, in his words "learning for emancipation."[8] It could even be argued that his dreams for adult education for the province were just as ambitious, just as far-sighted as those of Tommy Douglas. "The idea was to set up the structures that would enable people to act," Smith explained. "This is the point about participation ... getting the necessary information on which to act."[9]

This emphasis on providing opportunities for people was the genesis of the arts board concept. It also had much to do with Smith's view of the role and place of cultural activities in building a healthy society. As he bluntly noted, "Not to include the arts ... is to be more than a little bit stupid."[10] A provincial arts organization, according to Smith, was yet another way of facilitating and encouraging creativity—of providing the means by which people could be given the chance to express themselves artistically or participate in cultural activities.

Smith took his proposal to Woodrow Lloyd, minister of education in the Douglas cabinet. Although Lloyd at the time was largely preoccupied with the change to larger school units, he looked favourably upon the idea of an arts board and how it complemented the setting up of regional libraries. So, too, did Tommy Douglas, whose office door was always open to civil servants and their ideas. The premier concluded that an arts board would fill a yawning void in Saskatchewan: "I've always maintained that the people on the prairies ... are hungry for what are commonly described as things of the mind and spirit."[11]

The provincial climate could not have been better for Smith's proposal. Several artists and academics at the time were calling for greater support for authors, musicians, and the like so that they had a chance to realize their potential in Saskatchewan rather than leave, never to return, as others had done before. When painter Ernest Lindner appeared before the federal Massey Commission a few years later, he lamented how "the vast majority of the talented youth of the Province never is discovered, never has a chance of developing their potentialities and they land up in an uncongenial bread and butter profession."[12]

Smith drew up a draft set of guidelines for the board in several all-night sessions with Morris Shumiatcher, the premier's legal counsel.[13] The document was a clear reflection of Smith's views: that the creativity of Saskatchewan people was an untapped natural resource and that the role of the new government agency was to provide the means by which this creativity achieved full artistic expression. In other words, the board was to be an initiator in the first instance but, over time, become more of an enabler.[14]

Smith insisted that the new board be completely autonomous even though the board's budget would come from the provincial treasury. To this end, the draft guidelines gave the board complete control over the development of policies and programs, while administrative and management matters would be the responsibility of the Adult Education Division. This arrangement, from Smith's experience, was absolutely crucial to the board's functioning and ultimate success.[15]

The Saskatchewan Arts Board quietly came into existence on 3 February 1948 by means of order-in-council. It's not clear why the Douglas government chose that route. But what the document lacked in length, it made up for in reach. The new Saskatchewan Arts Board was to provide the province's citizens "greater opportunity to engage in creative activities … and to establish and improve the standards for such activities in the province."[16] A little more than one year later, the Saskatchewan Legislature passed an actual Arts Board Act.[17]

David Smith left Saskatchewan in 1953 to serve with UNESCO in Thailand as an adult education expert. He then returned to Simcoe County in 1959 and worked out of Barrie, Ontario, as a consultant to various agencies and organizations on all kinds of social issues. In his later years, he devoted his energies to peace and disarmament, a cause that largely preoccupied him up until his death at age ninety-four in 2006.

Smith's role in founding the Saskatchewan Arts Board was recognized in 1989 when the agency awarded him a Lifetime Award for Excellence in the Arts. He was proud of the distinction, but even prouder of the arts board itself, for he genuinely believed that the board was equal to any of the Douglas government's other initiatives.[18]

Through outreach programs, workshops, provincial tours, and exhibitions, the Saskatchewan Arts Board contributed to the development of new and emerging artists and at the same time generated public awareness and interest in their work—this in a province where in 1948 there had been "little professional arts activity... and many organizations operated without staff."[19] As David Smith's daughter reflected on the sixtieth anniversary of the agency, "If there was a little hesitancy initially it soon moved to enthusiasm."[20]

Stanley Smith

It was a charity case. The young, sickly boy, not yet ten, was lying in a Winnipeg hospital ward, facing the horrible prospect of losing his leg.

A few years earlier, Tommy Douglas had fallen and cut his knee on a stone while playing in his home village, Falkirk, Scotland. The wound failed to heal properly and osteomyelitis, a painful inflammation of the bone, had set in. A local doctor tried to get rid of the disease by operating on Tommy's leg on the family's kitchen table while his mother and grandmother assisted. But the painful scraping of his femur was not a success. The infection flared up from time to time, oozing pus, and making him ill.

Immigrating to Canada with his family in 1911, Tommy spent months in and out of hospital, undergoing treatment to try to fix his leg. And when he was not in hospital, he was hobbling around his Winnipeg neighbourhood on crutches or being pulled around in a small sleigh in winter. He would later call these years "the most unhappy period of my life." [1]

Eventually, Tommy's doctors recommended the amputation of the leg and gave the family time to think about it. There seemed to be little choice, especially when Tommy's parents could not afford the services of a specialist. That's when fate intervened.

An orthopaedic surgeon was going through the wards at Children's Hospital one day and, after examining Tommy's leg, proposed to take on the case as a teaching project for his students. Tommy's parents were anxious to do whatever they could to help their son and readily agreed, even though they were warned that the boy might lose movement in his knee. The operation, however, was a great success.

In his reminiscences with Chris Higginbotham more than half a century later, Tommy recalled that he had been treated by "a very famous orthopaedic surgeon, Dr. R. J. Smith." Tommy's childhood memory was extremely good, apart from the fact that the surgeon's name was actually Dr. Stanley Alwyn Smith.[2] And he may not have been all that famous at the time, but he was unusually skilled and exceedingly generous—the right man in the right place at the right time.

Born 12 November 1882, in Cheadle, Staffordshire, England, Stanley Alwyn Smith was the son of Lieutenant-Colonel T. J. Smith, a veterinary surgeon, and Jane Ellen Thomas of Crewe. Stanley was educated at Repton School, Derbyshire, one of the most famous of the co-educational "public schools" dating back to 1557.

Smith went to Edinburgh to study medicine, graduating with a Bachelor in Medicine (M.B.) and Bachelor in Surgery (B.Ch.) at only twenty-three in 1905.[3] He then obtained high-profile appointments, in turn, as house surgeon, senior house surgeon, and then assistant to Sir Robert Jones, one of the leading orthopaedic surgeons in the English-speaking world, at Royal Southern Hospital, Liverpool.[4] Smith's assigned tasks included demonstrating anatomy to the medical students at Liverpool University and giving anaesthetics at the hospital.

Few medical graduates in Britain possessed Smith's zeal for gaining additional education. There, unlike in North America, a doctorate degree in medicine resulted only after additional study and presentation of an acceptable thesis. Smith returned to his alma mater, Edinburgh, and was granted the M.D. degree in 1908 based on his thesis, "The differential diagnosis of some conditions of the hip joint with a few observations on the condition known as coxa vara."

Dr. Stanley Smith took on Tommy Douglas as a charity case and saved the young Winnipeg boy's leg from amputation. DR. IHOR MAYBA

It was even more exceptional to obtain an *additional* advanced degree. His second thesis, "Notes on certain of the rare derangements of the knee joint," earned him the degree of Master of Surgery (Ch.M.) in 1911. That same year, on 16 May, Smith passed his examinations to become a Fellow of the Royal College of Surgeons of Edinburgh.

Dr. Smith, a gifted orthopaedic surgeon, could have gone anywhere after his studies. He was ambidextrous—the rare ability to use both hands with equal facility—a great asset to a surgeon. He reportedly "had no superior and few equals in all Europe."[5]

But like thousands of other Britons in the early twentieth century, he decided that Canada offered a more promising future and headed to the bustling western Canadian city of Winnipeg, the so-called gateway to the Last Best West. Boasting a population of 136,000 at the time—a three-fold increase since the beginning of the century—the Manitoba capital's future seemed to be limitless and Smith wanted to be part of it.

On 16 October 1911, the newly qualified and exceedingly well-trained orthopaedic surgeon registered with the Manitoba College of Physicians and Surgeons.[6] How fortunate for many patients, but especially for Tommy Douglas. Over the course of slightly less than three years, Smith performed, without charge, at least three operations on young Tommy under anaesthetic, curetting out the infected bone and intermingled pus.

Smith remained in Winnipeg, building up a promising practice, for only three years before answering the call to duty. On 25 September 1914, less than one month after the outbreak of the Great War, he joined the Field Ambulance Corps of the Canadian Expeditionary Force with the rank of captain and was overseas by the end of the year.[7]

Smith served with distinction in France throughout 1915 and was twice mentioned in dispatches. He received the Distinguished Service Order for "conspicuous gallantry and devotion to duty at Festubert" on 20 May 1915: "Captain Smith, with a party of eight men, went out voluntarily to remove the wounded from an orchard whilst under heavy fire, and eventually succeeded in bringing all into safety.

Four of the eight men of the rescue party were wounded, and two of these have since died."[8]

In 1921, His Royal Highness Prince Arthur of Connaught conferred on Smith the [Officer of the] Order of the British Empire (OBE), a step higher than the coveted Member level (MBE). This distinction was given for "extraordinary skill in treatment of injured limbs, and in the fitting of artificial limbs, exercised in an invaluable degree during the war."[9]

Assigned to England, Smith was made surgeon-in-chief of Granville Canadians Special Hospital, Ramsgate, and placed in charge of all orthopaedic patients. One of the first things he did was write Pearl Evangeline Bradley, a well-trained American nurse who had worked with him at Children's Hospital in Winnipeg. She accepted his marriage proposal and made the dangerous boat trip across the Atlantic in 1916.[10]

Through the special intervention of his mentor Sir Robert Jones, Smith was next transferred to the British Army and placed in charge of Welsh Metropolitan War Hospital, Whitechurch, Cardiff, Wales. When the new Prince of Wales Orthopaedic Hospital was completed, Smith became the first trained and practising orthopaedic surgeon in South Wales. He supervised fitting of artificial limbs on 2,575 ex-servicemen. He was also in sole charge of teaching orthopaedics at the Welsh National School of Medicine in Cardiff, and simultaneously served as head of the Department of Orthopaedics at the Cardiff Royal Infirmary.

Smith had a respectable publication record. He wrote two chapters in orthopaedic textbooks, one of them edited by Sir Robert Jones. During his relatively short stay in Winnipeg, three articles appeared in the *Canadian Medical Association Journal* and two short notes in *Western Canada Medical Journal*. Smith also published four papers in *British Journal of Surgery*, three articles in *British Medical Journal*, two in *Lancet*, and one each in *Journal of Orthopaedic Surgery* and *Proceedings of the Royal Society of Medicine*. His article, "The diagnosis and treatment of injuries to the crucial ligaments,"[11] on the new process of opening the knee joint to repair injuries to the cruciate ligaments, was a "landmark" achievement, cited in the scientific literature thirty-five times between 1920 and 2003.

In 1926, not yet at the height of his career, Smith was stricken with what was then diagnosed as "Landry's paralysis," now known as Guillian-Barré Syndrome.[12] He was just forty-four. No longer able to perform orthopaedic surgery, he persevered as best he could under the shadow of gradual invalidism. He died at Pentyrch, west of Cardiff, on 22 February 1931.[13] His widow, Pearl, outlived him by thirty-seven years.

Sir Robert Jones wrote a fine appreciation of one of his most distinguished protegés: "He had all the qualities of an ideal surgeon—operative skill, a sense of proportion, sound judgement and resources, with a deep and abiding sense of responsibility, which made him a true guardian of the welfare of his patient. Orthopaedic surgery has indeed suffered a cruel blow."[14]

Tommy Douglas would have agreed. He never forgot how his leg would not have been saved if Dr. Smith had not agreed to take him on as a charity case. The experience would have a profound influence on his life. Tommy recalled, "I came to believe that health services ought not to have a price tag on them, and that people should be able to get whatever health services they required irrespective of their individual capacity to pay."[15] He was talking about what would become known as medicare.

Mark Talnicoff

He was, in many respects, Tommy Douglas's surrogate brother. Mark Talnicoff (later Talney) might have been five years older and from a Russian background, but he paired up with the scrawny immigrant kid from Scotland during their days in Winnipeg to become lifelong friends, even brothers-in-law through marriage.

What brought Mark and Tommy together was the church—and how it seemed to be failing society. Through their many discussions, they came to believe that organized religion had a moral duty to grapple with the many problems that plagued post-war Canada and help bring about a better world. "It wasn't enough to talk to people about some afterlife," Douglas recalled in his reminiscences. "We had to concern ourselves with the problems people had here and now … as Christians we can't be indifferent to how people live and what their daily problems are."[1] This thinking informed Douglas's ministry and later his politics.

Mark Alexander Talnicoff was born to Edward Talnicoff and Sofia Ricefield in Odessa, Russia, on 17 March 1899. The family fled from Odessa to New York to escape the 1905 pogrom[2] and later settled in Winnipeg about 1912.[3] Mark worked in wholesale dry goods sales,

Mark Talnicoff was Tommy's chum and roommate at Brandon College and a close friend and confidant. RON TALNEY

starting in 1915, and in his spare time acted as scoutmaster at Beulah Baptist Church in Elmwood, Winnipeg.[4]

That's where he met the fifteen-year-old Tommy Douglas, who had joined the Beulah congregation in 1919 and became a regular participant in the weekly church activities, especially the Tuesday night Scout meetings. Mark, with Tommy as his new assistant, organized a boys' bicycle group and "on summer weekends they would ride out to the country to camp under the stars. On Sunday morning they might attend a country church in their Boy Scout uniforms, and after church play some baseball with the local boys."[5]

This companionship made the pair close, almost like brothers, especially since Tommy had two younger sisters. And like most brothers, they talked about many things, particularly the world around them and how the Great War had shaken Canadian society to its very foundations.

Winnipeg in the early twentieth century was a kind of cultural crucible, populated by tens of thousands of "foreigners" from continental Europe—like the Talnicoffs—with strange customs, strange languages, even strange ways of dressing.[6] Because they were widely regarded as a threat to the British character of Canadian society, these immigrants faced discrimination, if not outright contempt. Tommy quickly learned, however, that immigrant families, whatever their ethnic origin, were just trying to get ahead like everyone else and that racism stood in their way. "They were wrestling with the same problems we were … trying to get established … trying to get jobs," he later observed, perhaps with people like Mark in mind. "You found that basically you were the same."[7]

Trying to make a decent living in post-war Winnipeg proved difficult for many workers, especially since their wages had not kept pace with the spiralling wartime inflation. In May 1919, tens of thousands consequently walked off their jobs as part of a general labour protest that effectively paralyzed the city for six weeks. The government, with the support of the business community, looked upon the work stoppage as a Bolshevik conspiracy and called on the Royal Northwest Mounted Police to brutally crush the strike.

Mark and Tommy personally witnessed the police action that day. On 23 June 1919, Bloody Saturday as it became known, the pair climbed atop a building to watch a showdown between the strikers and armed mounties on horseback. When demonstrators taking part in a protest parade failed to disperse when ordered, the police made three charges to clear the street, firing their guns into the crowd. One of the victims fell not far from the young men's viewing place.

Tommy was deeply troubled by the experience. "Certainly, as the years went by," Douglas recounted, "the Winnipeg General Strike left a very lasting impression on me ... Whenever the powers that be can't get what they want, they're always prepared to resort to violence ... to break the back of organized opposition." [8]

The Winnipeg General Strike was symptomatic of the problems that had accompanied the rapid urbanization and industrialization of Canada during the early twentieth century and then made worse by the Great War. And both Mark and Tommy, coming of age during these years, looked to the church for answers, if not direction. But Beulah Baptist Church was a conservative congregation—at least to the two Scout leaders—and they had trouble reconciling the emphasis on the afterlife that was being preached there with the troubles at hand. "Within the walls of that church," Mark remembered, "you readily forgot there was a world outside." [9]

The "young rebels," [10] as Mark and Tommy liked to see themselves, decided to work for the betterment of society through a more progressive gospel, one that applied the teachings of Jesus Christ to everyday life. To this end, the pair decided to enrol as ministry students at Brandon College, a liberal Baptist school west of Winnipeg. It was not until 1924, though, that they had saved enough money to get started, and even then, they had to work on the side to support themselves.

Despite the five-year age differential, Mark and Tommy were classmates and roommates during their first year of high school at Brandon Academy. They also took turns during the 1924–25 academic year preaching on alternate Sundays at the Baptist church in Austin and sometimes took a second service in the Forestville school northwest of Austin. As Tommy fondly recalled, at the Academy the pair "did any odd job, waiting tables or tending night-bells for students who came in late and got fined two-bits ... You kept the twenty-five cents for getting up and opening the door." [11]

Mark was undoubtedly a role model to the younger Tommy, as exemplified by his winning the Governor General's medal in the spring of 1925. He was also "a very loyal friend" according to Irma

Nan Douglas, age thirteen, got to know her future husband, Mark Talnicoff, through her brother Tommy. RON TALNEY

Dempsey, Tommy's future wife and fellow student.[12] But Mark was also "very sweet" on Tommy's sister Nan and "was around the [Douglas] house a lot" before he left for school in Brandon.[13] It was not really surprising, then, that he returned to Winnipeg, ostensibly to enter United Colleges (formerly Wesley College), but more important, to be closer to Nan.[14]

Mark and Nan were married in May 1927, and had their first child, Douglas Edward, in January 1929. While Mark completed his studies,[15] the couple lived alternately in the Douglas and Talnicoff homes. That's how Nan learned the art of Jewish-Russian cooking.

In 1930, Mark graduated with a B.A. (Liberal Arts), was ordained by the Manitoba Baptist Convention, and assumed charge of the Portage la Prairie First Baptist Church.[16] Tommy's story that year was almost identical. He graduated, was ordained, and secured his own church as well. But something else happened—Douglas married Irma Dempsey on 30 August. And the person who was called on to officiate at the wedding in the Dempsey boarding house in Brandon was Tommy's brother-in-law Mark.

Mark Talney served as pastor in Portage la Prairie until 1934 when he became executive secretary of the Student Christian Movement in Vancouver. In 1940, he left for the United States, changing his surname to Talney. He spent the next fifty years with the Presbyterian church in one capacity or another in Washington and Oregon. But he always kept one eye on what his "little brother" was doing north of the border as Saskatchewan premier and then leader of the New Democratic Party in Ottawa.

Talney died in Portland in December 1992, two years after the loss of his wife, Nan. Mark also outlived Tommy. As a testament to their friendship that spanned nearly seven decades, he prepared a poetic memorial ("Thomas Clement Douglas") published here for the first time:[17]

> Statesman
> Humanitarian
> adopted son of Canada,
> Scotland's heather
> clinging to him.
> By whose life
> the word compassion
> was made flesh.

His obsession,
to affirm the worth
and dignity of life—
every man's burden
his cross—
a voice
crying in the wilderness
of social injustice
for the voiceless.

Such stature
is not born—
it is made.
Nor did he stumble into it
denied other choices.
Such stature
is crafted
out of potentials
latent in human clay
pliant to Divine will
and purpose.
Face upward
he set his course
to a vast hope for mankind,
devoting to it
his words and works,
never swerving.
And when he fell,
it was to rise again
with undimmed vision,
renewing his dream-swept
heart
with firmer resolve.

He, who wore his many honors
with humble simplicity,
and sought no halo,
will live on
in the pages of the nation—
The Honorable T. C. Douglas.
In the memory
of multitudes of Canadians
he is Tommy Douglas—
the man who cared.

Malcolm Taylor

On 19 January 1947, thirty-two-year-old Malcolm Taylor stopped in Regina en route from the University of California, Berkeley, to an interim teaching position at the University of Toronto. It was not an idle, unplanned visit to the Saskatchewan capital. Taylor's Berkeley dissertation, titled "The Saskatchewan Hospital Services Plan," was still two years short of completion, and the doctoral student was curious to see first-hand how the CCF provincial government's nearly three-week-old hospital plan was functioning.

Taylor found the scene reminiscent of mobilization in 1939: "Clerks sitting elbow-to-elbow, processing the registration and tax collection payments according to a system that, although using mechanical tabulating equipment, was quite primitive." But even though "the staff were working under highly adverse conditions," he found that "their morale appeared extraordinarily high, all seeming to be inspired and excited by the challenge of the new enterprise." What struck Taylor during his brief stopover in Regina was how "a social idea had been translated into an operating reality: the first universal hospital insurance program in North America had been launched. For Saskatchewan, there was no turning back."[1]

Malcolm Taylor was research director for the Saskatchewan Health Services Planning Commission, the body that was charged with mapping the road to better public health and medical care in the province. SASKATCHEWAN ARCHIVES BOARD RWS-A11567

Malcolm Gordon Taylor, "educator, policy expert and activist ... a gentleman and a scholar,"[2] was born 31 August 1915 at Arrowhead, Alberta. He taught in rural one-room schools in Alberta during the difficult years of the Great Depression, but somehow managed to save enough money to go to Berkeley, California, where he graduated with a B.A. *(cum laude)* in 1942, M.A. (1943), and finally, a Ph.D. in political science in 1949.

Taylor's academic studies made him the perfect candidate for the position of research director for the Saskatchewan Health Services Planning Commission, the body that was charged with mapping the road to better public health and medical care in the province. His 1948 appointment to the commission gave the young scholar an opportunity to apply his academic training to the day-to-day practicalities of providing health care services. "It has been by design that these kind of people are around us," Premier Tommy Douglas boasted about his government's advisors and planners. "We give them a great deal of freedom in putting forth their ideas."[3]

Taylor's appointment was also timely. The government of Canada announced that same year that it would provide every province with funding to survey "present health services and facilities" in preparation for a national health insurance program.[4] Dr. Fred Mott, another Douglas recruit, who would serve as chair of the Saskatchewan Health Survey, asked Taylor to be his secretary and research director, effective January 1949. The Saskatchewan Health Survey (1949–51) consisted of a committee of twelve. There was one representative each from registered nurses, dentists, urban municipalities, rural municipalities, labour, the hospital association, the farmers' union, and the Swift Current Health Region. There were also two medical doctors: G. G. Ferguson, registrar of the Saskatchewan College of Physicians and Surgeons, and C. J. Houston, a general practitioner-surgeon from Yorkton. It was the job of Mott and Taylor to bring the work of this diverse but amicable group to a successful conclusion.

Mott's adroit chairing abilities,[5] coupled with Taylor's research skills, persuaded the committee to embrace procedures that emphasized co-operation. Although dealing with controversial topics, the group considered each issue in turn and hammered it out to the point of consensus. No minority report was submitted, nor were interim reports supplied to the organizations that each member represented.

After more than two years' work and no less than twenty-five meetings, the committee issued a two-volume committee report that contained a full catalogue of Saskatchewan health resources and an estimate of needs in the future. It also made 115 recommendations; the first was that "a comprehensive health insurance program should be undertaken at the earliest possible date."[6]

Ken McTaggart, summarizing the committee results for the Canadian Medical Association, declared that the report surpassed that for any other province and described it as "the classic of such projects."[7] Committee member Clarence Houston was equally pleased with the process. He told the Saskatchewan College of Physicians and Surgeons that the committee "established a precedent in working out health matters. It has proved that a widely representative type of Commission can work."[8]

Houston no doubt felt this way, in part, because of the work of Malcolm Taylor during the committee meetings. The pair became lifelong friends.[9] Taylor, in turn, was a great admirer of the medical profession and the many doctors with whom he met and worked. He recognized the profession's "sense of idealism and collective social good," which had "produced the best health care system in the world."[10]

When the Saskatchewan Health Survey was wrapped up in 1951, Malcolm Taylor left Saskatchewan, mission accomplished. He served as advisor to the Canadian Medical Association's Committee on Economics from 1953 to 1955 before being named the first principal of the University of Calgary (1960–64). In that position, he guided the institution's passage from a satellite campus of the University of Alberta to a full-fledged university, complete with professional colleges. This workload would have been demanding for most people, but during the same period, he acted as research consultant to the Hall Commission (1961–64), appointed by Diefenbaker to advise on a national health plan.

Taylor's next posting was as inaugural president of the University of Victoria (1964–68), where he once again grappled with the growing pains of a young institution.[11] His last academic appointment was as professor of public policy at York University, followed by retirement in Victoria, BC, in 1990. He died there in September 1994.

Taylor was the author of several books,[12] including his influential book, *Health Insurance and Canadian Public Policy* (1978, 1988), which won the Hannah Book Medal from the Royal Society of Canada.[13] The book was scrupulously fair to both doctors and politicians alike. So, too, was his delightful exposé, written on Saskatchewan medicare's thirtieth anniversary in 1992, which detailed the errors made by both sides in Saskatchewan that led to the bitter doctors' strike in 1962 and the dramatic rescue by Lord Stephen Taylor.[14]

Today, although Tommy Douglas is rightly remembered as the Father of Medicare, Malcolm Taylor was there as a kind of midwife, serving as a key member of the Saskatchewan Health Survey that recommended that the province adopt a comprehensive health insurance program.[15] Such a role is not surprising for a person who spent the better part of his life "assuring full and complete health care for every Canadian," regardless of who they might be or where they might come from.[16]

Notes

~≋~

Chapter One: Bill Baker

1 Lewis H. Thomas, ed., *The Making of a Socialist: The Recollections of T. C. Douglas* (Edmonton: University of Alberta Press, 1982), 322–23.

2 A. W. Johnson, *Dream No Little Dreams: A Biography of the Douglas Government of Saskatchewan, 1944–61* (Toronto: University of Toronto Press, 2004), 159–60.

3 H. R. Baker, "Baker, William B. (1919–1969)," *The Encyclopedia of Saskatchewan* (Regina: Canadian Plains Research Center, 2005), 85–86.

4 P. F. Rein, "These Changing Conditions: A Study of the Saskatchewan Royal Commission on Agriculture and Rural Life," (unpublished M.A. thesis, University of Regina, 1984), 57.

5 Thomas, ed., *The Making of a Socialist,* 325.

6 Johnson, *Dream No Little Dreams,* 226–28.

7 *Saskatoon Star-Phoenix,* 13 May 1964.

8 Thomas H. McLeod and Ian McLeod, *Tommy Douglas: The Road to Jerusalem* (Edmonton: Hurtig Publishers, 1987), 173.

9 Quoted in Rein, "These Changing Conditions," 171.

10 Thomas, ed., *The Making of a Socialist,* 324.

Chapter Two: Fred Bard

1 Fred McGuinness, e-mail, 27 October 2008.

2 Fred Bradshaw, *Report of the Game Commissioner, 1928* (Regina: J. W. Reid, King's Printer, 1928), 33.

3 Quoted at www.royalsaskmuseum.ca/about/museum_history_directors

4 In June 1940 the museum quarters in the Normal School had been taken over

by the British Commonwealth Air Training Plan. The museum moved into the former General Motors Parts and Service building until this building, too, was taken for wartime use. In June 1941 the museum office was moved into the Philips Glass Company building across the street on Toronto Street, where the museum staff had only one office and a small storeroom; the display cases had to be dismantled and put in unheated storage space. [Annual Report, Saskatchewan Natural Resources]. In December 1944 the museum was able to move back to the Normal School, but the display cases required much restoration and it did not open until 11 January 1946.

5 C. Stuart Houston, then a family practitioner in Yorkton.

6 Cruickshank wrote "Nature Notes" in the *Regina Leader-Post* for twenty years. *A Second Look: Liz Roley's Nature Notes* (Regina: Regina Branch of the Media Club, 1976). Liz Roley Cruickshank had played a key role as liaison of the Local Council of Women to the On-to-Ottawa trekkers in 1935. She was inducted as a Member of the Order of the British Empire (MBE) in 1948 and received an Honorary LL.D from the University of Regina in 1980. Anthony Jo, "Cruickshank, Elizabeth (1895–1989)," *The Encyclopedia of Saskatchewan* (Regina: Canadian Plains Research Center, 2005), 225.

7 Lewis H. Thomas, ed., *The Making of a Socialist: The Recollections of T. C. Douglas* (Edmonton: University of Alberta Press, 1982), 320.

8 Lahrman worked for the museum for fifty-five years. Lorne Scott, "Lahrman, Frederick William (1921–2003)," *Encyclopedia of Saskatchewan* (2005), 527-28.

9 Symons spent his summers on his ranch, "Hope Springs," in a mountain valley near Fort St. John, Alberta, depicted in his 1970 book, *The Broken Snare* (Toronto: Doubleday, 1970). Merle Massie, "Symons, Robert David (1898–1973)," *Encyclopedia of Saskatchewan*, 921. Born in Sussex, England, Symons came to Canada at the age of sixteen in 1914 to work on a ranch near Maple Creek. He was a game warden from 1926 to 1941. He wrote award-winning books and received an honourary degree from the University of Regina in 1970. *Many Patrols: Reminiscences of a Game Warden*, R. D. Symons (Regina: Coteau Books 1994), ix, 1.

10 Fred McGuinness, e-mail, 27 October 2008.

11 Michael Anthony Fedyk, "Pioneer Narratives as an Aspect of Collective Memory During the Saskatchewan Golden Jubilee," (unpublished M.A. thesis, University of Regina, October 2005).

12 "... the upkeep of pioneer dedication on the Royal Saskatchewan Museum has been all but ignored and the dedication is now obscured by dirt and debris. If pioneers still meant something similar to what they meant in the 1950s, the dedication would not have been permitted to enter the Centennial year in such a deplorable condition." Fedyk, "Pioneer Narratives," 41, fn. 11. Saskatchewan Archives Board (SAB) photograph # R-B4760.

13 Fedyk, "Pioneer Narratives," 12.

14 H. G. Deignan, "Proceedings of the Seventy-Seventh Stated Meeting of the American Ornithologists' Union," *Auk*, 77 (1960), 56–72.

Chapter Three: Allan Blair

1   Quoted in P. Krause, *Acts of Love: A Memoir* (Regina: Coteau Books, 1997), 231.
2   Florence M. Warriner, "Wilson Family," 742–44 and "Florence (Wilson) Blair Warriner," 746–47, in *Indian Head: History of Indian Head and District* (Indian Head, Sask: History of Indian Head and District Inc., 1984).
3   Quoted in Krause, *Acts of Love*, 76.
4   J. Brown, *Good Morning Susan: The Life and Times of Dr. Joe Brown* as told to Shelley Johnson (Regina: Oak Tree Publishing, 1986), 83.
5   Quoted in Krause, *Acts of Love*, 62–63.
6   *Saskatchewan Archives Board*, Allan Walker Blair curriculum vitae (courtesy Charles Hayter).
7   *Ibid.*
8   Brown, *Good Morning Susan*, 83.
9   C. S. Houston, *Steps on the Road to Medicare: Why Saskatchewan Led the Way* (Montreal/Kingston: McGill-Queen's University Press, 2002),106-8.
10 C. R. R. Hayter, "Compromising on Cancer: The Saskatchewan Cancer Commission and the Medical Profession, 1930–1940," *Saskatchewan History*, 54, 1: (2002), 14.
11 The new wing to the Grey Nuns Hospital in Regina was "the first building deliberately designed and constructed for no other purpose than the treatment of cancer." The story of cancer control in Saskatchewan has previously been recorded in David A. E. Shephard, "First in Fear and Dread—Cancer Control in Saskatchewan: A History of the Saskatchewan Cancer Commission, 1929–1979," unpublished MS, 1982.
12 Quoted in Krause, *Acts of Love*, 25.
13 *Ibid.*
14 The period from 1944 to 1959 was "a golden age ... a high point in Saskatchewan's program to control cancer." (Shephard: chapter 5, p. 3).
15 *Regina Leader-Post*, 10 November 1948.
16 *Ibid.*
17 Blair was also remembered by his posthumous portrait by artist Nicholas de Grandmaison. Brown, *Good Morning Susan*, 86.

Chapter Four: Brandon College Teachers

1   Lewis H. Thomas, ed., *The Making of a Socialist: The Recollections of T. C. Douglas* (Edmonton: University of Alberta Press, 1982), 41.
2   The Brandon College ministerial committee book entry for Douglas reads: "Baptized May 22 by Rev. F.R. Julian. Converted in 1917 in Scotland; worked in Mission. Came back to Canada in 1919 and joined Beulah Church Wpg ... the committee voted ... that he be put on 'encouraged' list." *Brandon College Archives*, series 10, Ministerial Committee Book, 27 March 1925.
3   Thomas, ed., *The Making of a Socialist*, 20, 39.

4 "Tommy Douglas, the Greatest Canadian," *Brandon University Alumni News,* v. 106, n. 1, spring/summer 2005, 8–9.

5 MacNeill, the son of a Baptist minister, born in Paisley, Ontario, in 1871, had been a member of the first graduating class from McMaster University, where he received a B.A. in Classics in 1894. He was a fixture at Brandon College. He began teaching Greek and Latin in 1903, then obtained his Ph.D. at the University of Chicago in 1910, and returned to Brandon to add New Testament Studies to his teaching load through 1930. As if that were not sufficient, he held additional responsibilities as dean of arts, 1912–30, and acting president, 1924–27.

6 The Baptist Church heresy hearing reaffirmed "the right of every man to read [the New Testament] by the light of God shining in his own heart" and "the refusal to apply any doctrinal test by either political or ecclesiastical authority." *Tommy Douglas: The Road to Jerusalem,* Thomas H. McLeod and Ian McLeod (Edmonton: Hurtig Publishers, 1987), 22.

7 Thomas, ed., *The Making of a Socialist,* 51.

8 McLeod and McLeod, *Tommy Douglas,* 22.

9 Now spelled "Chengdu."

10 C. S. Houston, *Steps on the Road to Medicare: Why Saskatchewan Led the Way* (Montreal/Kingston: McGill-Queen's University Press, 2002), 7–8. The interview was held 18 February 1983.

11 McLeod and McLeod, *Tommy Douglas,* 20.

12 *Ibid.,* 23.

13 Thomas, ed., *The Making of a Socialist,* 50.

Chapter Five: Bill Burak

1 J. Feather, "From Concept to Reality: Formation of the Swift Current Health Region," *Prairie Forum,* 16, no. 1, (spring 1991), 72.

2 "William James Burak," in *Treasured Memories Unfold: Rural Municipality of Stanley 215,* (Fenwood, Sask: RM Stanley History Book Committee, 1992), 321–22.

3 Feather, "From Concept to Reality," 69.

4 *Ibid.*

5 RM Pittville (1941 population of 1,193) and RM Riverside (1,701) shared the costs of Dr. A. L. Caldwell's $2,700 salary. Pittville, because of its smaller population, contributed less than half of the doctor's annual income. Caldwell resided in Cabri (RM Riverside).

6 Burak proudly enumerated this divergence as points 3, 4, 5, and 6 in his presentation on behalf of RM Pittville to the Sigerist Health Services Survey Committee in Regina on 26 September 1944 (*Saskatchewan Archives* Board, R251, f. 2, Sigerist brief #24, RM Pittville No. 169). However, when Burak mentioned to Sigerist that the Pittville health plan had been operating since 1937, he failed to clarify that this was merely the standard salaried municipal doctor system for the first four years. The unorthodox plan became operative only after Caldwell's departure.

7 Despite Burak's representations, Pittville's payments were ultra vires. The discrepancy required a change in legislation and hence Pittville's plan and that of RM Miry Creek No. 229 both persisted without legal status for over three years until the Swift Current Health Region #1 was inaugurated on 1 July 1946.

8 Sigerist brief #24, p. 3.

9 Burak told Sigerist in his brief that during seven years only six Pittville babies had been born away from hospital.

10 See Feather, "From Concept to Reality," 72–74 for a description of Burak's promotional activities.

11 Of 11,737 ballots, 8,154 were in favour, 3,392 against, and 191 ballots were spoiled. "History of the Swift Current Health Region Medical Care Plan, Research and Planning Branch," Sask. Health, June 1969, 7. "Out of his own pocket [Burak] had paid for all stamps, stationery, telephones, travelling and all other expenses." Munt, "How Swift Current Health Region was organized," 2.

12 C. S. Houston, *Steps on the Road to Medicare: Why Saskatchewan Led the Way* (Montreal/Kingston: McGill-Queen's University Press, 2002), 78–82. The British Parliament had passed a National Health Insurance Act in 1912, which came into effect in 1914. It was for wage earners only, not for the entire population.

13 Appended to Pittville RM Council minutes, 9 February 1946.

14 William J. Burak, *Our Ancestors* (Aberdeen: William J. Burak, 1974); available online as an electronic resource, University of Saskatchewan Library, CB201. B87 1974eb, bibliography, 582–91.

15 Lester Jorgenson, "Rural Municipality of Miry Creek No. 229 and Health Region No. 1," in *Bridging the Centuries* (Abbey, SK: Miry Creek Area History Book Committee, 2000), 52–58.

Chapter Six: George Cadbury

1 A. W. Johnson, *Dream No Little Dreams: A Biography of the Douglas Government of Saskatchewan, 1944–1961* (Toronto: University of Toronto Press, 2004), 71.

2 Quoted in *Ibid.,* 74.

3 R. I. McLaren, "The Saskatchewan Practice of Public Administration in Historical Perspective," *Canadian Studies*, 19 (1998), 100.

4 Quoted in J. Richards and L. Pratt, *Prairie Capitalism: Power and Influence in the New West* (Toronto: McClelland and Stewart, 1979), 130.

5 B. Bilson, "William J. Patterson" in G.L. Barnhart, ed., *Saskatchewan Premiers of the Twentieth Century* (Regina: Canadian Plains Research Center, 2005), 135.

6 *Time*, 14 January 1946.

7 Johnson, *Dream No Little Dreams*, 120.

8 McLaren, "Saskatchewan Practice," 101.

9 *Ibid.*

10 Richards and Pratt, *Prairie Capitalism*, 130.

11 *Ibid.,* 131.

12 *Time*, 24 June 1946.

Chapter Seven: Irma Dempsey

1 Thomas H. McLeod and Ian McLeod, *Tommy Douglas: The Road to Jerusalem* (Edmonton: Hurtig Publishers, 1987), 24.

2 Tommy had preached Sundays at Austin, Manitoba, during 1924–25, alternating weekends with his fellow high school student and (future) brother-in-law Mark A. Talnicoff; then at Carberry Presbyterian for two years, 1925–27; then at the combined Baptist charge of Shoal Lake–Strathclair (misspelled "Strathclare") for two years, 1927–29. Lewis H. Thomas, ed., *The Making of a Socialist: The Recollections of T.C. Douglas* (Edmonton: University of Alberta Press, 1982), 46. Austin was forty-nine miles east of Brandon. Strathclair was twenty-eight miles west of Minnedosa and Shoal Lake eight miles farther (*Waghorn's Guide* #839, November 1953).

3 *Waghorn's Guide*, 1929. Carberry was only twenty-eight miles east of Brandon. Two coast-to-coast trains came through every day, augmented by two more trains that came daily except Sunday. All four trains stopped at Carberry as well as Brandon, but only the "slow" trains stopped at Austin, another twenty-one miles east beyond Carberry. Even the slow train took only forty-eight minutes from Brandon to Carberry. The fare in 1929 was 95 cents one way. The trains left Brandon eastward at 4:35 and 8:15 A.M., and 1:40 and 5:10 P.M. The westward train left Carberry at 1:30 and 11:37 A.M., and at 3:53 and 9:12 P.M.

4 Other reports from that time were remarkably similar: "… a petite, brown-haired Methodist with shining eyes who came to hear him one Sunday and quickly changed churches." Dave Margoshes, *Tommy Douglas: Building the New Society* (Lantzville, BC: Quest Books, XYZ Publishing, 1999), 33; "… a slim, dark-haired, vivacious girl …" Walter Stewart, *The Life and Political Times of Tommy Douglas* (Toronto: McArthur & Co., 2003), 63.

5 McLeod and McLeod, *Tommy Douglas*, 28.

6 Telephone interview, John Oussoren with Stanley Knowles, 11 February 1990.

7 Doris French Shackleton, *Tommy Douglas: A Biography* (Toronto: McClelland and Stewart, 1975), 31.

8 McLeod and McLeod, *Tommy Douglas*, 2.

9 Telephone interview, John Oussoren with Irma Douglas, 12 and 13 February 1990.

10 Stewart, *The Life*, 68.

11 McLeod and McLeod, *Tommy Douglas*, 182. As regent of Sir Frederick Haultain chapter of the Imperial Order Daughters of the Empire (IODE), Mrs. Douglas gave leadership to a large group of Weyburn war workers. *Regina Leader-Post*, 14 September 1944.

12 *Regina Leader-Post*, 14 September 1944.

13 Stewart, *The Life*, 167.

14 Thomas, *Recollections*, 340–41.

15 *Ibid.*, 261–62, 388 (endnotes 8 and 9). The jury's judgement, rendered in Prince Albert under Mr. Justice George E. Taylor, was against the Tucker suit, but was appealed to the Appeal Court and the Supreme Court of Canada.

16 Irene Spry, Introduction to McLeod and McLeod, *Tommy Douglas*, x.
17 Thomas, *Recollections*, 315–16.
18 McLeod and McLeod, *Tommy Douglas*, 182.
19 *Ibid.*, 44.
20 Stewart, *The Life*, 302.

Chapter Eight: Sylvia Fedoruk

1 Fedoruk was also a member of the McKee rink that won the first showdown between winners of the eastern and western Canadian women's curling teams in 1960. She was inducted into the Canadian Curling Hall of Fame in 1986.
2 Thirty-eighth Annual Convocation, University of Saskatchewan, 12 and 13 May 1949.
3 Quoted in C. S. Houston, *Steps on the Road to Medicare: Why Saskatchewan Led the Way* (Montreal: McGill-Queen's University Press, 2002), 111.
4 *Ibid.*, 116.
5 See P. Litt, "Photo Finish: The Race to Build the Bomb," *The Beaver* (April–May 2002), 28–31.
6 Fedoruk, "The Growth of Nuclear Medicine" (1989), http://www.cns-anc.ca/history/fiftyyears/fedoruk.html
7 Dr. Ivan Smith, head of the second largest cancer clinic in Ontario, at London, was trained as a surgeon and as a pathologist, but not as a radiation therapist. Peter Monro, "Cobalt-60: A Canadian perspective. Part 3: London, Ontario and the "Peacetime Bomb, *Canadian Medical Physics Newsletter* 45 (1999), 64–68.
8 Houston, *Steps*, 120.
9 *Ibid.*, 153, n. 37.
10 Doug Cormack, Ed Epp, and Lloyd Bates were Fedoruk's fellow graduate students.
11 Houston, *Steps*, 120–22.
12 The ingenious dose collimator was built by John MacKay of Acme Machine and Electric in Saskatoon. The Picker X-ray Company sold cobalt-60 machines, with the MacKay collimator, around the world. Between AECL and Picker, cobalt-60 machines were the work horses around the world, especially—to this day—in underprivileged countries.
13 Fedoruk also modified a Reed Curtis scanner to register a photoscan and worked with physicist Trevor Cradduck in designing Canada's first gamma camera, thereby publishing the first images of isotope liver scanning in the world's most prestigious medical journal, the *New England Journal of Medicine*. Donald A. Fee and Sylvia O. Fedoruk, "Clinical value of liver photoscanning," *New England Journal of Medicine* 262 (1960), 123–25.
14 Fedoruk was inducted into the Canadian Medical Hall of Fame in 2009.
15 During the Roy Romanow premiership, Saskatchewan was the only province where the lieutenant-governor and the premier held monthly meetings.
16 D.Sc., University of Windsor, 1987, and University of Western Ontario, 1990;

LL.D., University of Regina, 1991, and University of Saskatchewan, 2006; D.Hum.L., Mount St. Vincent University, 1993.

17 *Canadian Who's Who*, 2001 et seq. (Toronto: University of Toronto Press, 2001), 415–16.

Chapter Nine: George Ferguson

1 C. S. Houston, *Steps on the Road to Medicare: Why Saskatchewan Led the Way* (Montreal/Kingston: McGill-Queen's University Press, 2002), 45.

2 Houston, *R.G. Ferguson, Crusader Against Tuberculosis* (Hannah Institute & Dundurn Press, 1991), 51, 86, 124–25.

3 Houston, *Steps*, 41.

4 This was a world first. C. S. Houston, "D.A. Stewart, 1874–1937: Western Tuberculosis Pioneer," *Annals of the Royal College of Physicians and Surgeons* 25:36–38.

5 Houston, *R.G. Ferguson*, 29.

6 Houston, *Steps*, 56.

7 *Ibid.*, 43.

8 *Ibid.*, 47, 50–51.

9 *Ibid.*, 52–53.

10 *Ibid.*, 56–60.

11 *Ibid.*, 53–55.

12 T. C. Douglas speech given at fiftieth anniversary of Saskatchewan Anti-tuberculosis League in 1961, quoted in Houston, *Steps*, 64.

Chapter Ten: Ertle Harrington

1 D. V. Cormack, "The Saskatchewan Radon Plant" in J. E. Aldrich and B. C. Lentle, eds., *A New Kind of Ray: The Radiological Sciences of Canada* (Vancouver: University of British Columbia Press, 1995), 391–92.

2 C. S. Houston and S. O. Fedoruk, "Radiation Therapy" in Aldrich and Lentle, eds., *A New Kind of Ray*, 142.

3 Quoted in *Ibid.*, 142.

4 C. R. R. Hayter, "Compromising on Cancer: The Saskatchewan Cancer Commission and the Medical Commission, 1930–40," *Saskatchewan History*, 54,1: (2002), 5.

5 *Ibid.*, 6.

6 Houston and Fedoruk, "Radiation Therapy," 142.

7 Cormack, "The Saskatchewan Radon Plant," 392.

8 Hayter, "Compromising on Cancer," 8. Harrington also sought the advice of another faculty member, chemist J. T. W. Spinks, who would go on to become university president.

9 Quoted in *Ibid.*, 9.

10 D. V. Cormack, "The Saskatchewan Radon Plant" in Aldrich and Lentle, eds., *A New Kind of Ray*, 391–94. After a year, with the radiation almost totally ex-

pended, the gold in the inactive seeds was sold to the Royal Mint in Ottawa, returning a little revenue to the Cancer Commission.

11 The gold functioned correctly only when metallurgically "fine" or almost 100 percent pure. This allowed the tubing to be sealed off by pinching the tubing with a pair of dull side cutters. Never did even the tiniest amount of radon escape from the radon seed thus formed. However, once when gold tubing of the "next best grade" arrived, the tubing would not seal off at all. Douglas V. Cormack to C. S. Houston, personal communication, 6 April 2009.

12 Elsewhere in the English-speaking world, to the best of our knowledge, full-time cancer physicists worked closely with radiotherapists only in Manchester, England, and New York City.

13 D. V. Cormack, "Allan W. Blair, E. L. Harrington and the Development of Medical Physics in Saskatchewan," *Canadian Medical Physics Newsletter*, 44 (1998), 78–80.

Chapter Eleven: Orville Hjertaas

1 J. Feather, "From Concept to Reality: Formation of the Swift Current Health Region," *Prairie Forum*, 16, no. 1, (spring 1991), 73.

2 *Ibid.*, 74

3 O. K. Hjertaas, "Report of Regional Organizer for months of October & November 1945." *Saskatchewan Archives Board* [*SAB*], Saskatchewan Department of Health, file 14-6-7.

4 *Ibid.*, 1.

5 *Ibid.*

6 *Ibid.*, 2.

7 *Ibid.*, 3.

8 *Ibid.*, 5.

9 *Ibid.*, 4.

10 *Ibid.*, 3.

11 Mindel C. Sheps, "Memorandum regarding health regions," *SAB*, Saskatchewan Department of Health, file 14-6-7, Health Services Planning Commission, undated, probably January 1946.

12 Following the positive vote in the southwest on 26 November 1945, favouring a full-service medical and hospital plan in Health Region #1, and before the government order-in-council of 11 December formally authorized its formation, Drs. Hjertaas and Sheps met with its organizing committee (Karl Kjorven, Walter Melrose, and Bill Burak) on 4 December 1945. C. S. Houston, *Steps on the Road to Medicare: Why Saskatchewan Led the Way* (Montreal/Kingston: McGill-Queen's University Press, 2002), 79–80; Sheps, "Memorandum," 1; *Gull Lake Advance*, 7 February 1946 (courtesy Joan Feather).

13 The inaugural meeting at Gull Lake occurred less than two months after the region, with the exception of a few municipalities along its eastern edge (which were thereby excluded), had voted on 26 November 1945 for Bill Burak's much more ambitious project for a complete prepaid health and hospital plan. At Gull

Lake were sixty-three representatives from sixty municipalities, twelve visitors and two newspaper reporters (Hjertaas, "Regional Board Meeting," 1.)

14   *SAB*, file 14-6-7, Orville K. Hjertaas, "Regional Board Meeting at Gull Lake, January 17 [1946], 2:00 P.M.

15   *Ibid.*, 1.

16   Mary MacIsaac lived to be 112. Independent and self-sufficient, she was regularly seen walking everywhere until the final two years of her life. She left behind six children, nineteen grandchildren, and twenty-nine great-grandchildren. She died on 10 March 2006. *Saskatoon Star-Phoenix*, 14 March 2006. She attributed her good health and longevity to eating oatmeal porridge every morning.

17   Millie Hjertaas, personal communication, November 2008.

18   Gordon S. Lawson, "Orville K. Hjertaas (1917–98)," *The Encyclopedia of Saskatchewan* (Regina: Canadian Plains Research Center, 2005), 447. The Prince Albert Community Clinic operated in rented quarters for two years until their new building was ready for occupancy in mid-1964.

Chapter Twelve: Kiyoshi Izumi

1   E. Dyck, "Kiyoshi Izumi and Mental Hospital Designs," *The Annual Bulletin for the Institute for Economic and Cultural Studies*, 18, (April 2008), 71–87.

2   F. H. Kahan, *Brains and Bricks* (Regina: White Cross Publications, 1965), 47–50.

3   *University of Saskatchewan Archives*, Kiyoshi Izumi curriculum vitae, 6 June 1948.

4   Dyck, "Kiyoshi Izumi," 78.

5   Quoted in *Ibid.*, 79.

6   *Ibid.*, 80.

7   F. H. Kahan, *Brains and Bricks*, 25–27, 36, 61.

8   The Yorkton Psychiatric Centre, costing $2,537,000, opened in October 1963 with Dr. G. Anthony Ives as superintendent.

9   Kahan, *Brains and Bricks*, 64–65, 135.

10   Saskatchewan spent $9.12 per capita on mental health, compared to $6.32 in British Columbia, $5.67 in Ontario, $5.55 in Alberta, and $4.28 in Manitoba. Further, Saskatchewan bore the highest cost of mental care (94.3 percent) as compared to 81 percent in Alberta and 79.6 percent in Manitoba. Letter from T. C. Douglas to Archdeacon F. E. R. Badham, president of the Saskatchewan Division of the Canadian Mental Health Association, 1 March 1961.

11   Dyck, "Kiyoshi Izumi," 72, 74.

Chapter Thirteen: Harold Johns

1   For the full account of the interview and the circumstance behind it, see C. S. Houston, *Steps on the Road to Medicare: Why Saskatchewan Led the Way* (Montreal/Kingston: McGill-Queen's University Press, 2002), 5–7.

2   Martin W. Johns, *Bamboo Sprouts and Maple Buds: Memoirs of a Life Begun in*

West China and Transplanted to Canada in 1925. (Hamilton: Copy Center of McMaster University, 1992); Martin W. Johns, *Sugaring Off: in which the Bamboo Sprouts take root in Canadian Soil.* (Hamilton: Copy Center, McMaster University Student Union, 1996).

3 Houston, *Steps*, 7.

4 C. S. Houston and S. O. Fedoruk, "Radiation Therapy in Saskatchewan," in *A New Kind of Ray: The Radiological Sciences of Canada,* eds. J. E. Aldrich and B. C. Lentle (Vancouver: University of British Columbia, 1995), 146.

5 C. L. Greenstock, "From Szechuan to Saskatchewan," in *A New Kind of Ray*, eds. Aldrich and Lentle, 247. H. E. Johns and C. Garrett, "Sensitivity and exposure graphs for radium radiography. *Canadian Journal of Research* 26A (1948), 292–305.

6 Houston and Fedoruk, "Radiation Therapy," 144, 146. See also Douglas V. Cormack, "Allan W. Blair, E. L. Harrington and the Development of Medical Physics in Saskatchewan." *Canadian Medical Physics Newsletter* 44 (1998), 78–80.

7 The element cobalt has an atomic weight of 59. But when cobalt is "cooked" in a nuclear reactor, it acquires another neutron—hence the name, cobalt-60. This new isotope emits powerful radiation, many times the radioactive power of radium.

8 Houston, *Steps*, 111.

9 Houston and Fedoruk, "Radiation Therapy," 144, 146.

10 Milford D. Schultz, "The Supervoltage Story," *American Journal of Roentgenology* 124 (1975), 541–49.

11 Houston, *Steps*, 115. Johns encouraged another of his graduate students, W. B. Reid, to develop a unique isotope brain-scanning device, that could demonstrate brain tumours. It was so far ahead of its time that it was used only in Saskatchewan, the Princess Margaret Hospital in Toronto, and the Montreal Neurological Institute. Only years later did the advent of microprocessor technology allow the technique to be used worldwide. S. O. Fedoruk, "The Growth of Nuclear Medicine," in *Special Symposium: Fifty Years of Nuclear Fission in Review.* Canadian Nuclear Society (10th annual meeting, Ottawa, 5 June 1989).

12 H. E. Johns and T. A. Watson, "The Cobalt-60 story," in *Cancer in Ontario 1982* (Toronto: Ontario Cancer Treatment and Research Foundation, 1982), 20–24.

13 One of his Saskatchewan graduate students, J. R. Cunningham, collaborated on the later editions. Johns also published over two hundred scientific papers and directly supervised sixty-five graduate students.

14 Including Fellow of the Royal Society of Canada, 1951; Roentgen Award of the British Institute of Radiology, 1953; Charles Mickle Fellowship, 1966; Henry Marshall Tory Medal, 1971; Coolidge Award, 1976; Gold medalist, American College of Radiology, 1980; and R. M. Taylor Award, 1983. He received four honorary degrees, an LL.D. from Saskatchewan in 1959 and three D.Sc.'s, from McMaster in 1968, Carleton in 1976, and Western Ontario in 1978.

15 J. Battista, "A night to remember—H. E. Johns inducted into the Canadian Medical Hall of Fame." *Canadian Medical Physics Newsletter* 45 (1999), 35–37.

16 When Johns received the prestigious Coolidge Award from the American

Association of Physicists in Medicine in 1976, he used the occasion to recall the time that he and Blair met with Douglas about the betatron. "By ten o'clock that morning we had [seen] the premier of the province, Tommy Douglas, whose enthusiasm matched ours, and whose permission gave us the full backing of the Saskatchewan government. I wonder if anyone could be so lucky today—to find a politician so eager to help." *Medical Physics* 3 (1976), 377.

Chapter Fourteen: Al Johnson

1 J. A. Mills and E. Dyck, "Trust amply recompensed: Psychological research at Weyburn, Saskatchewan, 1957–1961." *Journal of the History of Behavioral Sciences* 44 (2008), 201.
2 A. W. Johnson, *Dream No Little Dreams: A Biography of the Douglas Government of Saskatchewan, 1944–1961* (Toronto: University of Toronto Press, 2004), xviii.
3 During his career in Ottawa, Johnson served as assistant deputy minister of Finance (1964–68), economic advisor to the prime minister on the Constitution (1968–70), secretary of the Treasury Board (1970–73), deputy minister of National Welfare (1973–75), and president of the CBC (1975–82).
4 Johnson was the recipient of the Professional Institute of Public Service of Canada gold medal in 1975 and named a Companion of the Order of Canada, the highest rank in the Order, which recognizes individuals of international importance, in 1997.
5 Johnson, *Dream*, xxxiv.
6 G. P. Marchildon, foreword to *Dream*, xviii.
7 *Ibid.*, xv.
8 Publisher's "blurb" on back cover, *Dream*.

Chapter Fifteen: Stanley Knowles

1 Susan Mann Trofimenkoff, *Stanley Knowles, The Man from Winnipeg Centre* (Saskatoon: Western Producer Prairie Books, 1982), 20.
2 *Ibid.*, 26–38. The unjust treatment of Knowles's father, Stanley Ernest Knowles, by the Los Angeles Street Railway was never forgotten by his Canadian politician son. In the 1920s, the elder Knowles had spoken and written against jitney buses, the street railway's competition. In reward for this assistance, Knowles received his only week of paid holiday. But the company had no pension scheme, and when the depression hit in 1930, it cut his salary by 23 percent. When times became even tougher in 1932, twenty years of seniority counted for naught and they laid off their prized employee, together with all the others over fifty-five. The elder Knowles was fifty-seven and was forced to take a lower-paying job cleaning streetcars, back-breaking menial labour. He was soon in hospital with ulcers and died of cancer at age sixty-one.
3 *Ibid.*, 1–10.
4 *Ibid.*, 11–25.

5 Walter Stewart, *The Life and Political Times of Tommy Douglas* (Toronto: McArthur and Company, 2003), 60.

6 Knowles later served as chancellor of Brandon University, while the new student centre is called the Knowles-Douglas Student Centre.

7 Even though Knowles and Douglas had taken classes in religion, neither had a theology degree; a B.A. from a Baptist training institution was sufficient to officiate in a church. C. G. Stone and F. J. Garnett, *Brandon College, a History, 1899–1967* (Brandon: Brandon University, 1969), 131–32. Douglas had won the general proficiency medal in his final year of high school at the Brandon College Academy.

8 Knowles later claimed in a 1990 interview that he was not interested in the position, since he was not a Baptist, and that the church vote was really a matter of whether the congregation wanted Douglas. John Oussoren, "From Preacher to Politician: T.C. Douglas' Transition," (Doctor of Education thesis, University of Toronto, 1993), 103–04.

9 Lewis H. Thomas, ed., *The Making of a Socialist: The Recollections of T. C. Douglas* (Edmonton: University of Alberta Press, 1982), 54–55.

10 *Ibid.,* 81.

11 Because Knowles studied at a Baptist college, his name was included in a list of approved candidates for the Baptist ministry in the 1930 Year Book of the Baptist Union of Western Canada. Yet "he does not seem to have become a member of a Baptist church." Gerry Harrop, *Advocate of Compassion: Stanley Knowles in the Political Process.* (Hantsport, Nova Scotia: Lancelot Press, 1984), 152, n. 4.

12 Thomas, ed., *The Making of a Socialist,* 81.

13 *Ibid.,* 47.

14 Knowles was a CCF MP from 1942 through 1984, winning thirteen elections and losing only in 1958 during the John Diefenbaker sweep. From 1962 through 1972 he was chief whip and deputy leader of the NDP; he remained NDP house leader from 1972 until his cerebral hemorrhage in October 1981 (Harrop, *Advocate,* 123). In 1979, Knowles was named to the Privy Council. When he retired in 1984, Pierre Trudeau named him an honourary officer of the House, to sit at the centre table when the House was in session. He lived with multiple sclerosis from 1946 onwards; a stroke in 1981 restricted his subsequent activities. He was invested as an Officer of the Order of Canada in 1985. J. Trenaman, *Encyclopedia of Manitoba* (Winnipeg: Great Plains Publications, 2007), 369–70. He had never in his life weighed over 130 pounds (Harrop, *Advocate,* 22).

15 Thomas, ed., *The Making of a Socialist,* 65.

Chapter Sixteen: Sam Lawson

1 *Canadian Medical Association Journal* 103, (1970), 124. Incidentally, McKerracher and Lawson died four days apart. Both also served as president of the Canadian Psychiatric Association: McKerracher in 1955–56, Lawson in 1959–60.

2 J. A. Mills and E. Dyck, "Trust Amply Recompensed: Psychological Research at

Weyburn, Saskatchewan, 1957–1961," *Journal of the History of Behavioral Sciences* 44, no. 3 (summer 2008), 204.

3 "The Weyburn hospital stunk like something out of this world … the whole basement area was a shambles, naked people all over the place lying around, incontinent," said Lawson. J. A. Mills, "Lessons from the Periphery: Psychiatry in Saskatchewan, 1944-68," *History of Psychiatry* 18, no. 2 (2007), 197, n. 12.

4 J. A. Mills, "Lessons from the Periphery," 184; F. H. Kahan, *Brains and Bricks* (Regina: White Cross Publications, 1965), 82.

5 H. D. Dickinson, *The Two Psychiatries: The Transformation of Psychiatric Work in Saskatchewan* (Regina: Canadian Plains Research Center, 1989), 146–49.

6 F. S. Lawson, "Mental Hospitals: Their Size and Function," *Canadian Journal of Public Health* 49 (1958), 186–95.

7 Quoted in Dickinson, *The Two Psychiatries*, 152.

8 C. S. Houston, *Steps on the Road to Medicare: Why Saskatchewan Led the Way* (Montreal/Kingston: McGill-Queen's University Press, 2002), 149, n. 13.

9 Dickinson, *The Two Psychiatries*, 150–55.

10 Mills, "Lessons from the Periphery," 192.

11 Dickinson, *The Two Psychiatries*, 154; Mills, "Lessons from the Periphery," 185.

12 The CMHA was unusually powerful, with fifty-five thousand members in Saskatchewan alone. Almost certainly without precedent anywhere, Douglas and *each member of his cabinet* were members of CMHA (Mills, "Lessons from the Periphery," 183). This cosy relationship between CMHA and the CCF cabinet ceased abruptly in January 1957.

13 Lawson, on the executive of the CMHA, had an obvious conflict of interest. G. P. Marchildon, "Why was the CCF government in Saskatchewan so reluctant to adopt a community-based psychiatric system?" *Open Doors/Closed Ranks: Locating Mental Health after the Asylum Workshop* (presented at University of Saskatchewan, 22 August 2009).

14 Douglas wrote to J. Walter Erb, minister of Public Health, on 31 January 1957: "… no Government activity … has had … such a rapid increase in expenditure as the Psychiatric Branch … all the publicity from the Mental Health Association groups has been critical rather than helpful … some of our own employees are trying to blackmail the Government." *Saskatchewan Archives Board* (SAB), T. C. Douglas papers, R-33.1, XIV 572 (14–26), courtesy G. P. Marchildon. Roth pointed out to Douglas that "he had to swallow his rage because it would be well-nigh impossible to find a replacement for Lawson." Mills, "Lessons from the Periphery," 184–85, n. 34.

15 Dickinson, *The Two Psychiatries*, 163.

16 Not only did the medicalization of psychiatric work render the large mental hospitals technologically obsolete and economically unviable, but it also made the small community mental hospital redundant. *Ibid.*, 163. The 148 beds in the Yorkton Psychiatric Centre were already more than required when it opened on 30 September 1964.

17 *Ibid.*, 160–63.

18 Marchildon, "Why was the CCF," p. 11.

Chapter Seventeen: Hugh MacLean

1 Hugh MacLean, "An address on Medical Health Service," read at the CCF convention, Regina, 13 July 1944, *Saskatchewan Archives Board* (SAB), A69, file 2. Cited in Jacalyn Duffin, "The Guru and the Godfather: Henry Sigerist, Hugh MacLean, and the Politics of Health Care Reform in 1940s Canada," *Canadian Bulletin of Medical History/BCHM* 9 (1992), 191–218.
2 Letter from T. C. Douglas to Dr. Hugh MacLean, 6 November 1962. Cited in Duffin, "Guru and Godfather."
3 MacLean, "An address."
4 Lewis H. Thomas, ed., *The Making of a Socialist: The Recollections of T. C. Douglas.* (Edmonton: University of Alberta Press, 1982), 326.
5 Hugh MacLean to Henry E. Sigerist, 3 October 1944, *SAB*, A69, file 29. Cited in Duffin, "Guru and Godfather."
6 Duffin, "Guru and Godfather."

Chapter Eighteen: Wendell Macleod

1 Louis Horlick, *J. Wendell Macleod, Saskatchewan's Red Dean* (Montreal: McGill-Queen's University Press, 2007).
2 *Ibid.*, 4.
3 *Ibid.*, 20–24.
4 *Ibid.*, 34.
5 Quoted in *Ibid.*, 35.
6 Macleod practised with the Winnipeg Clinic from December 1945 through June 1952. Medical students held his teaching in high esteem, electing him the honorary president of the class that graduated in 1951 (C. S. Houston's class).
7 Horlick, *Macleod*, 41.
8 *Ibid.*, 135.
9 *Ibid.*, 42–67.
10 *Ibid.*, 46.
11 Quoted in *Ibid.*, 183.
12 Anne McDonald, "J. Wendell Macleod, 1905–2001." *The Encyclopedia of Saskatchewan.* (Regina: Canadian Plains Research Center, 2005), 571–72.
13 Horlick, *Macleod*, 66.
14 *Ibid.*, 57–67.
15 Macleod hired David Fish to establish a program of national statistical studies in medical education and to publish twenty-nine research reports. Macleod also played a part in the establishment of medical schools at Sherbrooke, Hamilton, and St. John's.
16 Macleod co-authored *Bethune: The Montreal Years, An Informal Portrait* in 1978, held a conference at McGill University in 1979 (the year that the People's Republic of China unveiled a large statue of Bethune at the corner of Guy and de Maisonneuve Streets in Montreal), and helped Dr. David Shephard edit and revise the publication of *Norman Bethune: His Times and His Legacy* in 1982.

17 Quoted in Horlick, *Macleod*, 66.

Chapter Nineteen: Vince Matthews

1 J. Feather, "Vincent Leon Matthews," *The Encyclopedia of Saskatchewan* (Regina: Canadian Plains Research Center, 2005), 581.
2 The Swift Current Health Region plan was financed by a personal tax—fifteen dollars for a single person, twenty-four dollars for two, thirty dollars for three, and thirty-five dollars for a family of four or more. There was also a property tax of 2.2 mills. In addition to the twenty-five-cent per capita subsidy, the provincial government also paid one-half the cost of x-rays, children's dental, and outpatient services, a total of $63,691 in 1948. C.S. Houston, *Steps on the Road to Medicare: Why Saskatchewan Led the Way* (Montreal/Kingston: McGill-Queen's University Press, 2002), 83.
3 Howden graduated from the University of Western Ontario in 1942. He later trained in ophthalmology at Saskatoon and then moved to practise in British Columbia.
4 Quoted in Houston, *Steps*, 86.
5 *Ibid.,* 82–83.
6 *Ibid.,* 85.
7 *Ibid.,* 84.
8 *Ibid.,* 82.
9 Quoted in *Ibid.,* 84.
10 Quoted in *Ibid.,* 86.
11 A. D. Kelly, "The Swift Current Experiment," *Canadian Medical Association Journal* 58 (1946), 506–11.
12 Joan Feather, "Impact of the Swift Current Health Region: Experiment or Model?" *Prairie Forum*. 16, no. 2 (fall 1991), 236, from *Maclean's Magazine*, 9 April 1960.
13 Thomas H. McLeod and I. McLeod, *Tommy Douglas: The Road to Jerusalem* (Edmonton: Hurtig Publishers, 1987), 150.
14 Lewis H. Thomas, ed., *The Making of a Socialist: The Recollections of T. C. Douglas* (Edmonton: University of Alberta Press, 1982), 372.
15 Matthews was acting deputy minister of Health, under Health Minister W. G. Davies from 30 June 1962 through 7 September 1962, then under Allan Blakeney through 1 September 1963, when J. G. Clarkson became deputy minister.
16 Feather, "Impact of the Swift Current Health Region," 239.

Chapter Twenty: Fred McGuinness

1 Lewis H. Thomas, ed., *The Making of a Socialist: The Recollections of T. C. Douglas* (Edmonton: University of Alberta Press, 1982), 317–18.
2 The full name of the Jubilee Act, passed March 1952, was *Bill No. 62—An Act to Provide for the Celebration of the Fiftieth Anniversary of the Establishment of the Province of Saskatchewan*. Michael Anthony Fedyk, "Pioneer Narratives as an

Aspect of Collective Memory During the Saskatchewan Golden Jubilee" (unpublished M.A. thesis, University of Regina, 2005), 14, n. 9.

3 *Ibid.*, 57.

4 Thomas, ed., *The Making*, 317.

5 Gerald A. Friesen, "An Interview with Fred McGuinness," *Manitoba History* 2:21–25.

6 Bill Redekop, "The sage in August: Fred McGuinness is the bridge between 'hicks' and 'slicks,'" *Winnipeg Free Press,* 28 September 2008. "I was raised in a Protestant nunnery," McGuinness said.

7 McGuinness, personal communication, 21 October 2008.

8 Douglas and McGuinness had a very special bond because they both suffered from osteomyelitis, and from flare-ups of osteomyelitis. For thirty years, McGuinness daily changed the dressings covering his draining sinus in his left thigh. The availability of penicillin and later of aureomycin made the disease easier to control. After thirty years of a draining sinus, a doctor prescribed unusually heavy doses of antibiotics for a week—and the pus finally stopped draining. Douglas's physicians would have been horrified to learn that when pain or fever or pus appeared, Tommy would phone McGuinness in the middle of the night, to ask for "a golden bullet from your fridge." McGuinness, who lived only a block away, remembers walking over with aureomycin capsules (his were paid for by the Canadian Department of Veteran Affairs), with Douglas waiting at his door to receive them and swallow one or two at once. Concern about development of antibiotic-resistant bacteria through such unprescribed use was many years in the future. McGuinness, personal communication, 27 October 2008.

9 Friesen, "An interview."

10 John Hall Archer had served in the Canadian Army, obtained his B.A. in history from the University of Saskatchewan and a library science degree from McGill University. He was appointed provincial archivist in 1948 and legislative librarian in 1950. Fedyk, "Pioneer Narratives," 55. Archer became the first president of the University of Regina, 1974–76 and received the Order of Canada in 1981 and Saskatchewan Order of Merit in 1987. He died 5 April 2004. J. Chaput, "Archer, John (1914–2004)," *The Encyclopedia of Saskatchewan* (Regina: Canadian Plains Research Center, 2005), 65.

11 McGuinness, personal communication, 15 October 2008. Culliton had been the Liberal member for Gravelbourg and Liberal finance critic, 1948–51. He had been narrowly defeated by Walter Tucker for the provincial Liberal leadership in 1946. Earlier, he had been the Liberal MLA for Gravelbourg, 1935–44, serving as provincial secretary, 1938–41, and minister without portfolio while in the Canadian Army, 1941–44. Brett Quiring, *Saskatchewan Politicians: Lives Past and Present* (Regina: Canadian Plains Research Center, 2004), 54–55.

12 Fedyk, "Pioneer Narratives," 57.

13 McGuinness, personal communication, 15 October 2008.

14 The book was named *Saskatchewan Harvest.*

15 Titled "The Face of Saskatchewan." Fedyk, "Pioneer Narratives," 122.

16 McGuinness, personal communication, 15 October 2008.

17 Irma Douglas's bran muffins were legendary. Colleen McGuinness, Fred's daughter, personal communication, 6 November, 2008, reports that her own reputation as a baker rests solely on the bran muffin recipe given her mother by Irma Douglas—the only bran muffin recipe that Mrs. McGuinness ever used.

18 McGuinness, personal communication, 27 October 2008.

19 160,000 tourists came to Saskatchewan in 1955. At least 25,000 were former residents. They came to 475 local Jubilee celebrations, some marked by civic holidays; three million people attended these events. The visitors spent an estimated five million dollars. Fedyk, "Pioneer Narratives," 9–10.

20 *Ibid.*, 72.

21 *Ibid.*

22 Redekop, "The sage."

23 *Ibid.*

24 *Ibid.*

Chapter Twenty-one: Griff McKerracher

1 E. Dyck, *Psychedelic Psychiatry: LSD from Clinic to Campus* (Baltimore: Johns Hopkins University Press, 2008), 19–20.

2 H. D. Dickinson, *The Two Psychiatries: The Transformation of Psychiatric Work in Saskatchewan* (Regina: Canadian Plains Research Center, 1989), 87.

3 L. H. Thomas, ed., *The Making of a Socialist: The Recollections of T.C. Douglas* (Edmonton: University of Alberta Press, 1982), 72.

4 Dyck, *Psychedelic Psychiatry*, 22–23.

5 Quoted in *Ibid.*

6 Quoted in Dickinson, *The Two Psychiatries*, 77–80. Hincks's recommendations paralleled those of the Sigerist report a year earlier. Both investigators recommended the forced sterilization of so-called "mental defectives"—a proposal that was never pursued by the Douglas government.

7 D. J. Buchan, *Greenhouse to Medical Centre: Saskatchewan's Medical School, 1926–78* (Saskatoon: College of Medicine, University of Saskatchewan, 1983), 183.

8 Dyck, *Psychedelic Psychiatry*, 25.

9 Dickinson, *The Two Psychiatries*, 141, figure 13.

10 *Ibid.*, 77, 140–144.

11 *Ibid.*, 92.

12 *Ibid.*, 110.

13 C. M. Smith et al., "Care of the Certified Psychiatric Patient in the General Hospital: The Saskatoon Project," *Canadian Medical Association Journal*, 88 (1963), 360–64.

14 C. M. Smith, "McKerracher, Donald Griffin (1909-1970)," *The Encyclopedia of Saskatchewan* (Regina: Canadian Plains Research Center, 2005), 586.

15 J. A. Mills, "Lessons from the periphery: psychiatry in Saskatchewan, Canada, 1944–68." *History of Psychiatry* 18 (2007), 182.

16 Colin M. Smith, personal communication, 22 March 2004.

17 McKerracher's scientific contributions included papers in *Canadian Medical Asso-*

ciation Journal, Canadian Journal of Public Health, Canadian Psychiatric Association Journal, Mental Hospital, Mental Hygiene, Wisconsin Medical Journal, The Lancet, and *The New England Journal of Medicine.* Topics included "The Family Doctor and the Psychiatric Ward," "Care of the Certified Psychiatric Patient in the General Hospital," "Psychiatry in General Practice," and "Patients Make Good Teachers."

18 Quoted in Thomas H. McLeod and Ian McLeod, *Tommy Douglas: The Road to Jerusalem* (Edmonton: Hurtig Publishers,1987), 155.

Chapter Twenty-two: Eleanor McKinnon

1 *Regina Leader-Post,* 3 March 1954.
2 Eleanor McKinnon interview, 2 October 1994.
3 Eleanor McKinnon interview, 14 November 1982.
4 Dr. Campbell retired three years later and died three months after that on 18 October 1947. *Canadian Medical Association Journal* 57 (1947), 606. McKinnon interview, 2 October 1994.
5 McKinnon interview, 2 October 1994.
6 McKinnon interview, 14 November 1982.
7 Thomas H. McLeod and Ian McLeod, *Tommy Douglas: The Road to Jerusalem* (Edmonton: Hurtig Publishers, 1987), 119.
8 McKinnon interview, 14 November 1982.
9 Quoted in *Regina Leader-Post,* 9 January 2004.
10 R. Tyre, *Along the Highway* (Regina: School Aids and Text Book Publishing Company, 1950), 34–35.
11 McKinnon interview, 2 October 1994.
12 *Regina Leader-Post,* 9 January 2004.
13 *Regina Leader-Post,* mid-1949 (Heading of two-column article with large headline: "Secretary of premier finds her job a whirl.")

Chapter Twenty-three: Norman McKinnon

1 It is worth noting that Weyburn's largest employer was the mental hospital, where many of the employees, from the janitor up, were patronage appointments of the Liberal political machine.
2 Weyburn was their destination because of encouragement from Neil McKinnon's sister. She was married to Dr. Robert Menzies Mitchell, one of Weyburn's pioneer medical doctors and a three-time Liberal member of the Saskatchewan legislature, 1908, 1912, and 1917. Mitchell served as superintendent of the new Saskatchewan Hospital in Weyburn from 1919 to 1930.
3 Henry Friesen, "Baptist Union of Western Canada," *The Encyclopedia of Saskatchewan* (Regina: Canadian Plains Research Center, 2005), 89–90.
4 Minutes, special meeting, Calvary Baptist Church, 22 September 1929. (Courtesy Rev. Douglas C. Loden).
5 Lewis H. Thomas, ed., *The Making of a Socialist: The Recollections of T.C. Douglas.* (Edmonton: University of Alberta Press 1982), 52–53.

6　In 1935, Douglas's weekly salary alternated between $30 and $28 from January to May, then the payments from June through August varied according to what the weekly collection permitted: $25, $20, $16, $25, $20, $25, $12, $12, $30, and $8.50, followed by $30 on September 24. (Calvary Baptist Church ledger, courtesy Rev. Douglas Loden).

7　Elsie Cross had come west to live with her sister, Mattie Leslie, the wife of Rev. R. S. Leslie, minister to the thriving congregation at Knox Presbyterian Church. Elsie worked in a real estate office, attended her brother-in-law's church, and met Norman McKinnon while ice-skating. Elsie and Norman were married in a private Presbyterian wedding on Rev. Leslie's farm, ten miles south and ten miles west of Weyburn, on 29 July 1909. Elsie was baptized as a Baptist on 29 March 1910.

8　Calvary Church minutes.

9　Thomas, ed., *The Making of a Socialist*, 52–53.

10　"Norman McKinnon dies suddenly in Regina Sunday," *Weyburn Review,* 10 September 1942, 1. The funeral was one of the largest ever held in Weyburn.

11　"McKinnons terminate long business career in Weyburn," *Weyburn Review,* 31 December 1942.

12　The Weyburn Co-op took over the ground floor of the McKinnon store in 1944 and then purchased the entire building in 1951. Isabel Eaglesham, *The Night the Cat Froze in the Oven: A History of Weyburn and its People* (Weyburn: Weyburn Review,1963), 161.

Chapter Twenty-four: Tommy McLeod

1　Thomas H. McLeod and Ian McLeod, *Tommy Douglas: The Road to Jerusalem* (Edmonton: Hurtig Publishers, 1987), 119.

2　*Ibid.,* 5.

3　*Ibid.,* 1.

4　Walter Stewart, *The Life and Political Times of Tommy Douglas* (Toronto: McArthur and Company, 2003), 74.

5　McLeod and McLeod, *Tommy Douglas*, 29.

6　A. W. Johnson, *Dream No Little Dreams: A Biography of the Douglas Government of Saskatchewan, 1944–1961* (Toronto: University of Toronto Press, 2004), 95.

7　*Ibid.,* 94.

8　*Ibid.,* 138.

9　Honours bestowed on McLeod included the Vanier Medal from the Institute of Public Administration in 1971 and the Order of Canada in 2003.

10　Stewart, *Life and Political Times,* 304.

Chapter Twenty-five: Arthur Morton

1　D. R. Murray and R. A. Murray, *The Prairie Builder* (Edmonton: NeWest Press, 1984), 161–62.

2　On 20 May 1941, the Royal Society of Canada awarded the [J. B.] Tyrrell Gold Medal to Dr. Morton, "teacher, scholar, archivist and historian." The citation described his "mastery of geographical detail, his biographical knowledge, and his acquaintance with the technique and processes of the human activities which have affected the West."

3 Thomas R. Barcus, "Arthur Silver Morton, 1870–1945," *The Library Journal,* 15 March 1945.

4 *Ibid.*

5 James F. Kenney, "Arthur Silver Morton, 1870–1945," *Proceedings of the Royal Society of Canada* (1945), 101.

6 Minutes of Council, University of Saskatchewan, 9 May 1945.

7 On 9 May 1941, the University of Saskatchewan conferred on Dr. Morton, "a sympathetic teacher, a meticulous scholar and a devoted advocate of the British faith," the honorary degree of Doctor of Laws, "for distinguished contributions to the historical study of Western Canada."

8 J. Champ, "Arthur Silver Morton and his Role in the Founding of the Saskatchewan Archives Board," *Archivaria* 32 (summer 1991), 101, 103.

9 Seventy-eight Orders-in-Council authorized destruction and only two allowed retention. *Ibid.,* 102–03.

10 Quoted in *Ibid.*, 103.

11 *Ibid.,* 104.

12 *Ibid.,* 109.

13 Thomas H. McLeod and Ian McLeod, *Tommy Douglas: The Road to Jerusalem* (Edmonton: Hurtig Publishers, 1987), 120.

14 *Ibid.*

15 Political scientist David Smith suggests that the "ease of access to a large selection of well-catalogued public and private records accounts in large part for the province's publishing record." Champ, "Arthur Silver Morton," 110.

16 Quoted in *Ibid.*

Chapter Twenty-six: Fred Mott

1 Thomas H. McLeod and Ian McLeod, *Tommy Douglas: The Road to Jerusalem* (Edmonton: Hurtig Publishers, 1987), 151.

2 L. H. Thomas, ed., *The Making of a Socialist: The Recollections of T. C. Douglas* (Edmonton: University of Alberta Press, 1984), 231.

3 A. W. Johnson, *Dream No Little Dreams: A Biography of the Douglas Government of Saskatchewan, 1944–1961* (Toronto: University of Toronto Press, 2004), 145.

4 Thomas, ed., *The Making of a Socialist,* 226.

5 *Ibid.*

6 Marjorie had married Mott in 1930. Her father, Canon William Bertal Heeney, was the rector of St. Luke's Anglican church in Winnipeg from 1909 to 1942. Her brother, Arnold Heeney, was educated at the University of Manitoba, taught at St. John's College there, and received a Rhodes scholarship. Arnold Heeney, *The Things that are Caesar's: Memoirs of a Canadian Public Servant* (Toronto: University of Toronto Press, 1972). Arnold became Mackenzie King's principal secretary in 1939, and in 1940 became clerk of the Privy Council and secretary

of the Liberal Cabinet in 1940. He co-ordinated the Cabinet War Committee, which gained him recognition as the most important civil servant in Ottawa during World War Two. Later, he was undersecretary of state for External Affairs, ambassador to the United States (and to NATO) and Canadian head of the International Joint Commission, as well as chair of the Canadian Civil Service Commission. J. M. Bumsted, *Dictionary of Manitoba Biography* (Winnipeg: University of Manitoba Press, 1999), 108.

7 M. G. Taylor, *Health Insurance and Canadian Public Policy* (Montreal: McGill-Queen's University Press, 1978), 103–04.

8 McLeod and McLeod, *Tommy Douglas*, 152.

9 *Ibid.*

10 Taylor, *Health Insurance and Canadian Public Policy,* 114, n. 84.

11 Johnson, *Dream No Little Dreams,* 146.

12 *University of Saskatchewan Archives,* Honorary Degree Recipients, Frederick Dodge Mott, 14 May 1955.

Chapter Twenty-seven: Humphry Osmond

1 Erika Dyck, *Psychedelic Psychiatry: LSD from Clinic to Campus* (Baltimore: Johns Hopkins University Press, 2008), vii, 2–3, 11, 14.

2 *Ibid.,* 15–17.

3 J. H. Tanne, "Humphry Osmond, Psychiatrist who investigated LSD, 'turned on' Aldous Huxley, and coined the word 'psychedelic.'" *British Medical Journal* 328 (1984), 713.

4 Telephone conversation between C. S. Houston and Robert Sommer, 29 November 2008.

5 Quoted in Dyck, *Psychedelic Psychiatry*, 24.

6 *Ibid.,* 25–28, 45–52. Hoffer became a leading proponent of orthomolecular medicine, using especially large doses of a vitamin, nicotinic acid. See Colin M. Smith, "Mental Health Services," *The Encyclopedia of Saskatchewan* (Regina: Canadian Plains Research Center, 2005), 599–601.

7 John A. Mills and Erika Dyck, "Trust amply recompensed: Psychological research at Weyburn, Saskatchewan, 1957–1961." *Journal of the History of Behavioral Sciences* 44 (2008), 201, 215.

8 The word *psychedelic* was introduced into the English lexicon by Osmond in "A Review of the Clinical Effects of Psychotomimetic Agents," *Annals of the New York Academy of Sciences* 66:418–434, in 1957. The two lines are from Erika Dyck, *Psychedelic Psychiatry,* 2.

9 Smith, "Mental Health Services," 600.

10 Dyck, *Psychedelic Psychiatry*, 36, 45.

11 *Ibid.,* 54, 62. Colin M. Smith, "A new adjunct to the treatment of alcoholism: the hallucinogenic drugs," *Quarterly Journal of Studies on Alcohol* 19 (1958), 406–17.

12 Dyck, *Psychedelic Psychiatry*, 70–71.

13 Kay Parley, *Lady with a Lantern* (Regina: Benchmark Press, 2007), 87.

14 *Ibid.*, 7. This was the American Psychiatric Association Achievement Award for "the most improved facility."

15 Dyck, *Psychedelic Psychiatry*, 113.

16 Tanne, "Humphry Osmond, Psychiatrist who investigated LSD," 713.

17 Together, Sommer and Osmond studied the altered spatial perceptions of mental patients. Robert Sommer and Humphry Osmond, "Autobiographies of Former Mental Patients," *Journal of Mental Science* 107 (1960), 648–62. Mills and Dyck ("Trust amply recompensed," 214) said of Weyburn, "freedom of action caused research to blossom."

18 Robert Sommer, "In Memoriam: Humphry Osmond," *Journal of Environmental Psychology* 24 (2004), 257–58, and personal communication, 28 November 2008.

19 Robert Sommer, "Action Research: From Mental Hospital Reform in Saskatchewan to Community Building in California, 4, 5 *In:* Invited address given at the annual meeting of the Canadian Psychological Association, Edmonton, 3–6 June 1998.

Chapter Twenty-eight: Stewart Robertson

1 Quoted in J. Feather, "Impact of the Swift Current Health Region: Experiment or Model," *Prairie Forum* 16, no. 2, (fall 1991), 226.

2 "Stewart and Agnes Robertson," *Prairie Memories* (Webb, Saskatchewan: Webb History Book Committee, 1982), 1068–69.

3 *Ibid.*, 1068.

4 Anonymous, "Medical Care and Health Region No. 1," *Prairie Memories*, 62.

5 The minutes of the RM of Webb (bylaw No. 86, 7 February and 31 March 1944) give the vote as 291 in favour and only 53 opposed.

6 Webb followed the March 1939 Municipal Medical and Hospital Services Act, also known as the "Matt Anderson Plan," whereby payments were made to doctors by the doctor-sponsored organization then known as Medical Services Incorporated and later as Group Medical Services. A fee of seven dollars per person or a maximum of fifty dollars was levied and all deficits were taken care of by mill rate.

7 Pat Cammer, "Some Memories of the Beginnings of Health Region #1," paper presented at Health Region #1 Remembrance Celebration, Swift Current, 3 June 1993, 10.

8 *Ibid.*, 11.

9 Despite the introduction of the Saskatchewan Hospitalization Plan, 94 percent of residents of the remainder of Saskatchewan waited more than thirteen years to obtain the full health care plan enjoyed by southwest residents during that time. The 1946 census showed a population of 53,597 in SCHR #1, compared to a Saskatchewan total of 832,688.

10 Expenditure for medical services within the region, on a fee-for-service basis, was $410,453 in 1947 and $453,925 in 1948. In 1948, doctors received an average gross revenue of $12,880—a net income averaging $8,114, since the overhead for a doctor in the area was estimated at 37 percent. Referrals to specialists out-

side the region, mainly Regina, came to $58,547 in 1947 and $67,909 in 1948. J. A. Matheson, O. M. Irwin, F. B. Dawson, and G. G. Ferguson, "Report of the Swift Current Health Region No. 1," *Saskatchewan Medical Quarterly* 11 (1947), 21–25.

11 Cammer, "Some Memories," 9.

12 Lester Jorgenson of RM Miry Creek #229 also insisted that the SCHR was a local, grassroots phenomenon. Although supported by the province, "the widely held concept that the Swift Current plan was a provincially-directed pilot project does not fit the recorded facts." L. Jorgenson, "Rural Municipality of Miry Creek No. 229 and Health Region No. 1" in *Bridging the Centuries* (Abbey, Saskatchewan: Miry Creek Area History Committee, 2000), 55.

13 Quoted in Feather, "Impact of the Swift Current Health Region," 238.

14 *Ibid.*, 234.

15 *Ibid.*, 244.

Chapter Twenty-nine: Tommy Shoyama

1 Quoted in Thomas K. Shoyama profile, Department of Finance web site (www.fin.gc.ca/comment/shoyama08).

2 *Globe and Mail*, 30 December 2006.

3 Lewis H. Thomas, ed. *The Making of a Socialist: The Recollections of T. C. Douglas.* (Edmonton: University of Alberta Press, 1982), 7.

4 *Globe and Mail*, 30 December 2006.

5 Thomas H. McLeod and Ian McLeod, *Tommy Douglas: The Road to Jerusalem* (Edmonton: Hurtig Publishers, 1987), 174.

Chapter Thirty: Morris Shumiatcher

1 In July 2005, Ahenakew was found guilty of wilfully promoting hatred toward Jews and fined one thousand dollars. But the conviction was overturned on appeal. A second trial was held in November 2008. This time Ahenakew was acquitted on the grounds that he did not have the requisite criminal intent of wilfully promoting hatred in a public place.

2 C. Patrias, "Socialists, Jews and the 1947 Saskatchewan Bill of Rights," *Canadian Historical Review* 87, no. 2, (June 2006), 278.

3 A. W. Johnson, *Dream No Little Dreams: A Biography of the Douglas Government of Saskatchewan, 1944–1961* (Toronto: University of Toronto Press, 2004), 125.

4 There are conflicting dates in the literature as to when exactly Shumiatcher joined the Saskatchewan civil service. *Who's Who* gives 1949 as his last year of work for Douglas.

5 Quoted in Patrias, "Socialists, Jews," 279.

6 Thomas H. McLeod and Ian McLeod, *Tommy Douglas: The Road to Jerusalem* (Edmonton: Hurtig Publishers, 1987), 120.

7 Ken Norman, "Saskatchewan Bill of Rights," *The Encyclopedia of Saskatchewan* (Regina: Canadian Plains Research Center, 2005), 798–99.

8 In its first year of office, the Douglas government had been "both innovative and courageous" in fighting racial discrimination. It granted Chinese-Canadian citizens the right to vote, and it specifically invited Japanese-Canadians to settle in Saskatchewan. The Department of Education distributed five thousand copies of a pamphlet, *The Races of Mankind,* "which debunked widespread misconceptions about race." Patrias, "Socialists, Jews," 274–75.

9 *Ibid.,* 277.

10 *Ibid.,* 271. Shumiatcher had contemplated running for the CCF in Alberta in 1944 because it was, he said, "The only party in which a Jew could rise to the top." (*Ibid.,* 278).

11 *Ibid.,* 272, 280. After 1945, the JLC, under the influence of David Lewis and his father, Maishe Lewis, re-oriented the JLC work "from fighting anti-Semitism to the promotion of human rights in Canada." (*Ibid.,* 272).

12 *Ibid.,* 280. Unfortunately, the section prohibiting discrimination based on sex was removed in the revision stage.

13 *Ibid.,* 265. Events have not borne out Corman's high hopes for the Bill of Rights. Seymour Lipset's *Agrarian Socialism* (Berkeley: University of California Press, 1950) makes no mention of it and Johnson's *Dream No Little Dreams* slights it.

14 *Ibid.,* 284, 288, 289.

15 *Ibid.,* 283, 286.

16 *Ibid.,* 292.

17 Norman, "Saskatchewan Bill of Rights," *Encyclopedia of Saskatchewan,* 798–99.

18 Daria Coneghan, "Shumiatcher, Morris Cyril" *Encyclopedia of Saskatchewan,* 859, and *Who's Who in Canada* (2001), 1182. Shumiatcher was made Officer of the Order of Canada in 1981 and received the Saskatchewan Order of Merit in 1997.

Chapter Thirty-one: Henry Sigerist

1 Quoted in L. Horlick, *They Built Better Than They Knew: Saskatchewan's Royal University Hospital, A History, 1955–1992* (Saskatoon: College of Medicine, University of Saskatchewan, 2001), 9.

2 Quoted in Thomas H. McLeod and Ian McLeod, *Tommy Douglas: The Road to Jerusalem* (Edmonton: Hurtig Publishers, 1987), 147.

3 Malcolm G. Taylor, *Health Insurance and Canadian Public Policy* (Montreal: McGill-Queen's University Press, 1978), 88, 434.

4 Quoted in Horlick, *They Built Better Than They Knew,* 9.

5 Quoted in *Ibid.,* 10.

6 Quoted in *Ibid.*

7 McLeod and McLeod, *Tommy Douglas,* 148.

8 Quoted in Horlick, *They Built Better Than They Knew,* 10.

9 Jacalyn Duffin and L. A. Falk, "Sigerist in Saskatchewan: the quest for balance in social and technical medicine." *Bulletin of the History of Medicine* 70 (1996), 683.

10 Horlick, *They Built Better Than They Knew,* Appendix A, 317.

11 C. S. Houston, *Steps on the Road to Medicare: Why Saskatchewan Led the Way* (Montreal: McGill-Queen's University Press, 2002), 69–81.

12 Professor Milton Roemer of the University of California, Los Angeles, nonethe-less described the Sigerist report as "one of the most advanced health services reports of its time." Joan Feather, "From concept to reality: formation of the Swift Current Health Region," *Prairie Forum* 16 (1991), 59.

13 Duffin and Falk, "Sigerist in Saskatchewan," 660, 683.

Chapter Thirty-two: Charlie Smith

1 Quoted in *Maclean's*, 1 January 2000.

2 "His passion for the human values of the CCF party was unmistakable … He was kind, considerate and compassionate; approachable and supportive; humor-ous and humble; empathetic and fair." Dave Anderson, *To Get the Lights: A Memoir About Farm Electrification in Saskatchewan* (Victoria: Trafford Publish-ing, 2005), 19–22.

3 *Ibid.*, 23.

4 In 1926, Smith's father built the short-lived River View Amusement Park in the South Saskatchewan River valley, twenty-five miles north of Swift Current.

5 C. O. White, *Power for a Province: A History of Saskatchewan Power* (Regina: Canadian Plains Research Center, 1976), 265. Only 1 percent of all farms in western Canada secured their electricity from power lines.

6 M. Barber, "Help for Farm Homes: The Campaign to End Housework Drudgery in Rural Saskatchewan in the 1920s," *Scientia Canadiensis* 9, no. 1 (1985), 3–26.

7 L. C. Volk, "The Social Effects of Rural Electrification in Saskatchewan," (un-published M.A. thesis, University of Regina), 1980, 89.

8 White, *Power for a Province,* 267.

9 *Ibid.*, 268.

10 Anderson, *To Get the Lights,* 118-26.

11 White, *Power for a Province,* 279.

12 *Ibid.*, 280.

13 Anderson, *To Get the Lights*, 191-2.

14 A brilliant name, using an appropriate power surname; the first name indicated that the lowest part of the power rate was one cent a kilowatt hour! Lillian Vigrass, a home economist from Pathlow, was inducted into Saskatchewan's Ag-ricultural Hall of Fame in 2001.

15 George Busse was Lillian's boss and Charlie Smith's best friend. While Lillian promoted use of electricity in the farmhouse, Busse promoted its use in the farmyard and fields. Busse has received insufficient credit for this work.

16 White, *Power for a Province,* 288; Anderson, *To Get the Lights,* 215.

17 White, *Power for a Province*, 284. It would take until 1965, when Regina handed over the keys to its powerhouse, before one single, integrated system was finally in place.

18 Volk, "The Social Effects of Rural Electrification in Saskatchewan," 170–78.

19 Quoted in R. Collins, *You Had To Be There* (Toronto: McClelland and Stewart, 1997), 201.

Chapter Thirty-three: David Smith

1 A. W. Johnson, *Dream No Little Dreams: A Biography of the Douglas Government of Saskatchewan, 1944–61* (Toronto: University of Toronto Press, 2004), 147.
2 Telephone interview with Sheila Roberts, 4 September 2009.
3 D. Smith, *First Person Plural: A Community Development Approach to Social Change* (Montreal: Black Rose Books, 1995), 118.
4 *Ibid.,* 152.
5 Roberts interview.
6 Smith, *First Person Plural,* vi.
7 *Ibid.,* 122.
8 *Ibid.,* 125.
9 *Ibid.,* 115.
10 *Ibid.,* 125.
11 Lewis H. Thomas, ed., *The Making of a Socialist: The Recollections of T. C. Douglas* (Edmonton: University of Alberta Press, 1982), 320–21.
12 Quoted in D. E. Smith, ed., *Building a Province: A History of Saskatchewan in Documents* (Saskatoon: Fifth House Publishers, 1992), 23. The Canada Council, the federal equivalent of the Saskatchewan Arts Board, was not created until 1957.
13 Roberts interview.
14 Smith, *First Person Plural,* 123.
15 Roberts interview.
16 Order-in-council 228/48, *Saskatchewan Gazette,* 14 February 1948.
17 See *Statutes of Saskatchewan,* c. 63, 1949.
18 S. Roberts, "Saskatchewan Arts Board," unpublished presentation, 6 February 2008 (copy provided by Roberts).
19 J. Morgan, "Saskatchewan Arts Board," in *The Encyclopedia of Saskatchewan* (Regina: Canadian Plains Research Center, 2005), 796.
20 S. Roberts, "Saskatchewan Arts Board."

Chapter Thirty-four: Stanley Smith

1 Thomas, Lewis H., ed., *The Making of a Socialist: The Recollections of T. C. Douglas,* (Edmonton: University of Alberta Press, 1982), 13.
2 Both his middle name, Alwyn, and his subsequent career in Wales, strongly suggest that he carried some Welsh blood in his veins. His three sons all chose to use the hyphenated surname, "Alwyn-Smith."
3 He registered with the General Medical Council of Great Britain on 28 July 1905.
4 Early during Smith's tutelage under Sir Robert Jones in 1906, the Mayo brothers of Rochester, MN, visited Liverpool. They hoped to initiate North America's first separate department of orthopaedic surgery, and planned to visit leading European centres that exemplified the best orthopaedic practice in the world.

They scheduled one day in Liverpool but stayed for a week, realizing that they had found the Holy Grail of orthopaedics. They sent one of their most promising young surgeons, Dr. Melvin Starkey Henderson, for a year of study with Jones. Henderson returned and initiated a separate orthopaedic department that followed exactly the methods of Sir Robert Jones. B. F. Morrey, "The influence of Sir Robert Jones on the founding and development of orthopaedic surgery at the Mayo Clinic." *Journal of Bone and Joint Surgery* 87-B (2006), 106–07.

5 Robert Phelps, *The Prince & the Pioneers: The Early Work of the Prince of Wales Orthopaedic Hospital* (Cardiff: University Hospital of Wales and Cardiff Royal Group of Hospitals, 1993), 37.

6 Smith joined in practice with Dr. Herbert P. H. Galloway, western Canada's first orthopaedic surgeon, at 611 Broadway Avenue, Winnipeg. Galloway, an Ontarian who had graduated from the University of Toronto in 1887, had also trained under Sir Robert Jones in Liverpool. Smith was promptly appointed orthopaedic surgeon to the Winnipeg Children's Hospital. When the Winnipeg Medical Society was formed 7 February 1913, Smith was elected its secretary-treasurer. *Western Canada Medical Journal* (1911), 528, (1913), 89, and (1914), 473, 479. I. I. Mayba, *Bonesetters and Others, Pioneer Orthopaedic Surgeons* (Henderson Books, Winnipeg 1991), 33, 80, 112–13, 200.

7 His physical examination 33237, 3 September 1914, by Dr. James S. Nelson, listed Smith as "Height 5 ft. 7 ins., eyes brown, chest expansion 35½ to 39 inches, scar right back." Library and Archives Canada. Soldiers of the First World War - CEF. RG 150, accession 1992-93/166, Box 9103-54.

8 *Supplement to London Gazette,* 25 August 1915, 8502.

9 Citation, OBE, Cardiff, 21 January 1920.

10 Pearl Bradley had originally hailed from Peekskill in Westchester, the prosperous county on the Hudson River immediately north of New York City. I. I. Mayba, *Bonesetters and Others: Pioneer Orthopaedic Surgeons.* (Winnipeg: Henderson Books, 1991).

11 *British Journal of Surgery* 6(22):176–89.

12 Letter from his son, Dr. Peter Alwyn-Smith to Dr. I. I. Mayba, 7 October 1985. Guillain-Barré Syndrome is an acute inflammatory polyneuropathy, today known to be an autoiummune disorder affecting the peripheral nervous system. However, the steadily progressive course of Alwyn Smith's condition would be more in favour of "motor neuron disease" or Amyotrophic Lateral Sclerosis (later popularly known as "Lou Gehrig's disease" after the American baseball player).

13 Officiating at Smith's funeral were the Very Reverend Garfield Williams, OBE, Dean of Llandaff Cathedral, the Very Reverend Canon A. Jones, vicar of Llandaff, three other clergy, and members of council and committees of the Prince of Wales Hospital. Smith was survived by his wife, who died 2 July 1968, and three sons. Son Robert died during active service in North Africa at age twenty-one; Michael served in the Canadian Navy, retired with the rank of lieutenant commander and then worked with the Canadian Department of Veterans' Affairs in Prince Edward Island; Peter was a family practitioner at Porthcawl, Glamorgan,

Wales (Mayba, *Bonesetters,* 81).

14 Jones, R., "Stanley Alwyn Smith, D.S.O." *British Medical Journal* 1 (March 1931), 425–56; *Who Was Who, 1929–1940* (London: Adams & Charles Black, 1947), 1257.

15 Thomas, ed., *The Making of a Socialist,* 7.

Chapter Thirty-five: Mark Talnicoff

1 Lewis H. Thomas, ed., *The Making of a Socialist: The Recollections of T.C. Douglas* (Edmonton: University of Alberta Press, 1984), 65–66.

2 R. Weinberg, "The pogrom of 1905 in Odessa: a case study," in *Pogroms: Anti-Jewish Violence in Modern Russian History,* eds., J. D. Klier and S. Lambroza (Cambridge: Cambridge University Press, 1992), 248–89. Of 140,000 Jews, 28 percent of the population of Odessa, with "an inordinate amount of wealth, power, and influence," at least four hundred were killed, three hundred injured, and sixteen hundred of their buildings damaged.

3 Mark Talney's sons were in their thirties before each learned independently of their Jewish origin. Ron ate a meal in a Jewish delicatessen and noted that the food served there, for one example, *kinish,* was almost identical with what his mother, Nan, had served regularly at home. His mother, Nan, then admitted that she had learned Jewish-Russian cooking from her mother-in-law in Winnipeg. Ron's brother Doug about the same time had learned from Canadian immigration, when he moved from California to a professorship in music at the University of British Columbia, that his grandfather's Canadian immigration papers had listed his racial origin as Jewish. Ron G. Talney, personal communication.

4 Mark was converted at the Mission of Tabernacle Church, Winnipeg, by a Miss Burroughs. *Brandon College Archives,* series 10, Ministerial Committee book, 27 March 1925.

5 Thomas H. McLeod and Ian McLeod, *Tommy Douglas: The Road to Jerusalem* (Edmonton: Hurtig Publishers, 1987), 17.

6 The family name in Odessa, Russia, was Spitalnicoff. Cousins in Cleveland called themselves Spitalny; Phil Spitalny (whose photograph bears a striking resemblance to Mark Talnicoff as senior stick in Winnipeg) was a composer of popular songs and the conductor of a famous All Girl Orchestra that performed on U.S. radio networks. See portrait on "Big Band Library: Phil Spitalny 'Charm School'" on www.cornslaw.net/allgirlorchestra

7 Thomas, ed., *The Making of a Socialist,* 14.

8 *Ibid.,* 32.

9 McLeod and McLeod, *Tommy Douglas,* 17.

10 *Ibid.*

11 Thomas, ed., *The Making of a Socialist,* 44.

12 Telephone interview, John Oussoren with Irma Douglas, 12–13 February 1990.

13 *Ibid.*

14 Nan, born in Falkirk, Scotland, 3 August 1908, was nine years younger than Mark.

15 At college, Talnicoff was on the editorial board of *Vox,* a thrice-yearly student

publication, on the winning debating team, and in his final year was Senior Stick (student body president).

16 *Presbyterian Historical Society Archives*, Biographical File RG 414: Mark A. Talney.

17 Reproduced with the kind permission of Mark Talney's son, Ronald Garth Talney.

Chapter Thirty-six: Malcolm Taylor

1 M. G. Taylor, *Health Insurance and Canadian Public Policy* (Montreal: McGill-Queen's University Press, 1978), 103–04, 435n81.

2 A. Paul Williams, "In tribute to Malcolm Gordon Taylor," *Health and Canadian Society*, 3, no. 1 & 2 (1995), 12.

3 Lewis H. Thomas, ed., *The Making of a Socialist: The Recollections of T. C. Douglas* (Edmonton: University of Alberta Press, 1982), 337.

4 Privy Council #3408. Saskatchewan was allotted $43,506 for this purpose.

5 According to later comments by C. J. Houston, Mott was a perfect chair. Mott first skilfully elicited the opinions of each member. Only then did he summarize what he saw as a solution. In a situation that might have engendered violent differences of opinion, Mott's method eliminated divisive confrontation among his individual members. C. S. Houston, "Saskatchewan Health Survey, 1949–51." *The Encyclopedia of Saskatchewan* (Regina: Canadian Plains Research Center 2005), 908–09.

6 Health Survey Committee, *Saskatchewan Health Service Report* (Regina, Department of Health, 1951), 225.

7 Ken McTaggart, *The first decade: the story of the birth of Canadian Medicare in Saskatchewan and its development during the following 10 years* (Ottawa: Canadian Medical Association, 1973), 43.

8 C. J. Houston, "Report," *Sask. Medical Quarterly* 15, no. 4 (1951), 626.

9 C. S. Houston, *Steps on the Road to Medicare: Why Saskatchewan Led the Way* (Montreal: McGill-Queen's University Press, 2003), 147n20.

10 Taylor was disappointed, however, whenever medical leaders showed a tendency to confuse the economic interests of the profession with the public interest. Williams, "In tribute to Malcolm Gordon Taylor," 11.

11 *Ibid.*, 9.

12 Taylor also wrote *The Administration of Health Insurance in Canada, The Financial Aspects of Health Insurance*, and *Insuring National Health Care: The Canadian Experience*.

13 Williams, "In tribute to Malcolm Gordon Taylor," 10.

14 M. G. Taylor, "Medicare turns 30," *Can. Med. Assoc. J.* 147 (1992), 233–37.

15 The citation on Taylor's honorary LL.D. from York University reads: "The present health of the nation, and the envy which Canada's health system arouses in many other countries, owes much to the efforts of Malcolm Taylor."

16 J. E. Boan, "Taylor, Malcolm Gordon, 1915–94." *Encyclopedia of Saskatchewan* (Regina: Canadian Plains Research Centre, 2005), 926.

Further Reading

———————— ⤬ ————————

C. S. Houston, *Steps on the Road to Medicare: Why Saskatchewan Led the Way* (Montreal/Kingston: McGill-Queen's University Press, 2002).

A. W. Johnson, *Dream No Little Dreams: A Biography of the Douglas Government of Saskatchewan, 1944–61* (Toronto: University of Toronto Press, 2004).

Dave Margoshes, *Tommy Douglas: Building the New Society* (Lantzville, BC: Quest Books, XYZ Publishing, 1999).

T. H. McLeod and I. McLeod, *Tommy Douglas: The Road to Jerusalem* (Edmonton: Hurtig Publishers, 1987).

Walter Stewart, *The Life and Political Times of Tommy Douglas* (Toronto: McArthur & Co., 2003).

L. H. Thomas, ed., *The Making of a Socialist: The Recollections of T. C. Douglas* (Edmonton: University of Alberta Press, 1984).

Bill Waiser, *Saskatchewan: A New History* (Calgary: Fifth House Publishers, 2005).

Please consult the endnotes for a more complete list of sources.

Acknowledgments

⚍

Just as Tommy Douglas benefited from the support, assistance, and encouragement of many individuals, so did we in the research, writing, and production of this book. We consider ourselves extremely fortunate to have received the kind help we did along the way.

Charlene Dobmeier of Fifth House Publishers was enthusiastic from the beginning about the book, in large part because she readily understood and appreciated our desire to tell another side of the Tommy Douglas legacy in Saskatchewan. Fraser Seely drew upon his intimate understanding of the book business to develop a handsome design.

Several people read the completed manuscript and provided valuable feedback and suggestions: Allan Blakeney, Desmond Morton, and Jim Miller. Naturally, any possible errors of interpretation or fact are our own.

Then, there are the dozens of people (listed alphabetically) who sent us research materials, did interviews, offered direction and advice, checked sources, secured photographs, corrected our writing, and generally did whatever they could to help with the project. We are deeply indebted to these individuals:

David Anderson, Rae Anderson, Cheryl Avery, Louise Ayotte, Roy Bailey, Jon Bath, Beth Bilson, Errol Bredin, Pola Burak, Michael

Carter, Nadine Charabin, Douglas V. Cormack, Jeanie Cyr, Ken Dahl, Vickie Lamb Drover, Jacalyn Duffin, Erika Dyck, Terry Erdelyan, Joan Feather, Hon. Sylvia Fedoruk, Mike Fedyk, Blair Galston, Kelly D. Garnett, Leesa Girouard, Brian Graham, Morna Greuel, Patrick Hayes, Charles R. R. Hayter, Chris Hives, Millie Hjertaas, Brian Hubner, Elisabeth Hugel, Edna Jen-Warrington, Martin W. Johns (deceased), Steven Kerr, David Knowles, Leah Koldingnes, Kelly Kozij, Pat Blair Krause, Dr. Bob Lampard, Mrs. Sadie Lampard, Gordon Lawson, Dr. Brian C. Lentle, Rev. Douglas Loden, Matt Lowe, Dr. Peter Macleod, Dwain Main, Greg Marchildon, Kim Marschall, Lieutenant Colonel A. F. Matheson, Maureen Matthews, Mrs. Pat Matthews, Dr. Ihor Mayba, Colleen McGuinness, Fred McGuinness, John A. Mills, Tom Mitchell, Dr. Bernard F. Morrey, Anne Morton, Greg Nikkel, Ken Norman, Tim Novak, Rev. John Oussoren, Gabrielle Prefontaine, Skippy Raines, Kristina Rissling, Dr. Alun Roberts, Sheila Roberts, Ruth Robinson, Jude Romualdo, Lorne Scott, Penny Shaw, David A. E. Shephard, Eileen Meyer Sklar, Dr. Colin M. Smith, Dr. Robert Sommer, Connie Sorenson, Jill Sutherland, Margot Talney, Ronald G. Talney, Shelly Thierman, Dr. O. L. Wade, Deanna Waters, Rachel Wells, Nola Zinn.

Some of the production costs were covered by a generous grant from the President's Publication Fund at the University of Saskatchewan.

Finally, we owe a special thank-you to our partners, Mary Houston and Marley Waiser, who probably lived with the book as much as we did and never tired of hearing about the people behind Tommy or listening to the latest story we uncovered. This book is warmly dedicated to them.

About the Authors

C. Stuart Houston received his M.D. from the University of Manitoba in 1951, specialized in radiology, and taught at the College of Medicine, University of Saskatchewan, 1955–96, where he was head of the department of medical imaging from 1982 to 1987. Best noted for his studies of aboriginal children, he edited the *Journal of the Canadian Association of Radiologists* for five years.

He has received numerous awards as an ornithologist and conservationist. A Fellow of the American Ornithologists' Union, he edited the memorials in *The Auk* for twenty-one years. A bird bander since 1943, he and his subpermittees have banded over 140,000 birds of 209 species, with a record 3,350 recoveries. A past president of the Canadian Society for the History of Medicine, he has written eleven books and co-edited the health sector articles for the *Encyclopedia of Saskatchewan* (2005).

He received a D.Litt. from the University of Saskatchewan in 1987, the Saskatchewan Order of Merit in 1992, was made an Officer of the Order of Canada in April 1993, and has been in *Canadian Who's Who* since 2001.

Bill Waiser, a specialist in western and northern Canadian history, joined the Department of History at the University of Saskatchewan in 1984 and served as department head from 1995 to 1998. He was Yukon Historian for the Canadian Parks Service prior to his university appointment.

Bill has published several books, including the award-winning centennial history of the province, *Saskatchewan: A New History*. A regular commentator in print, radio, and television, he hosted a weekly history segment, "Looking Back," during the early evening news broadcast on CBC Saskatchewan TV.

Bill was named the university's Distinguished Researcher at the spring 2004 convocation and received the College of Arts and Science Teaching Excellence Award in 2003. He was awarded the Saskatchewan Order of Merit, the province's highest honour, in 2006 and elected a fellow of the Royal Society of Canada the following year.

Bill is a recreational runner who likes to garden, hike, and canoe.

Index